T0312283

Cambridge Elements ≡

Elements in Soviet and Post-Soviet History
edited by
Mark Edele
University of Melbourne
Rebecca Friedman
Florida International University

MAKING NATIONAL DIASPORAS

Soviet-Era Migrations and Post-Soviet Consequences

Lewis H. Siegelbaum
Michigan State University

Leslie Page Moch
Michigan State University

CAMBRIDGE
UNIVERSITY PRESS

Shaftesbury Road, Cambridge CB2 8EA, United Kingdom

One Liberty Plaza, 20th Floor, New York, NY 10006, USA

477 Williamstown Road, Port Melbourne, VIC 3207, Australia

314–321, 3rd Floor, Plot 3, Splendor Forum, Jasola District Centre, New Delhi – 110025, India

103 Penang Road, #05–06/07, Visioncrest Commercial, Singapore 238467

Cambridge University Press is part of Cambridge University Press & Assessment, a department of the University of Cambridge.

We share the University's mission to contribute to society through the pursuit of education, learning and research at the highest international levels of excellence.

www.cambridge.org
Information on this title: www.cambridge.org/9781009371834

DOI: 10.1017/9781009371810

First published 2023

A catalogue record for this publication is available from the British Library.

ISBN 978-1-009-37183-4 Paperback
ISSN 2753-5290 (online)
ISSN 2753-5282 (print)

Making National Diasporas

Soviet-Era Migrations and Post-Soviet Consequences

Elements in Soviet and Post-Soviet History

DOI: 10.1017/9781009371810
First published online: July 2023

Lewis H. Siegelbaum
Michigan State University

Leslie Page Moch
Michigan State University

Author for correspondence: Lewis H. Siegelbaum, siegelba@msu.edu

Abstract: This Element explains the historical conditions for the seemingly anomalous presence of people outside of "their own" Soviet republic and the sometimes fraught consequences for them and their post-Soviet host countries. The authors begin their inquiry with an analysis of the most massive displacements of the Stalin era – nationality-based deportations – concluding with examples of the life trajectories of deportees' children as they moved transnationally within the Soviet Union and in its successor states. Section 2 treats disparate parts of the country as magnets attracting Soviet citizens from far afield. Most were cities undergoing vast industrial expansion; others involved incentive programs to develop agriculture and rural-based industries. Section 3 is devoted to the history of immigration and emigration during the Soviet period as well as since 1991, when millions left one former Soviet republic for another or for lands farther afield.

Keywords: migration, diasporas, Soviet, Russia, post-Soviet

ISBNs: 9781009371834 (PB), 9781009371810 (OC)
ISSNs: 2753-5290 (online), 2753-5282 (print)

Contents

Introduction

One of the Russian state's key justifications for its intervention in Ukraine in 2014 and massive military invasion of that country in 2022 has been to rescue the Russian population in Ukraine's eastern region and thereafter extend to it the benefits of the "Russian world." Many have debated whether these people needed rescuing, regarding Russia's actions as nothing but naked aggression. But why, it may be asked, are people identified as Russian living in Ukraine? How did they get there? When did they arrive? It turns out that, as Figure 1 illustrates, millions of Russians have been living outside of the territory defined as Russia. In 1989, 25.2 million, more than one in every six Russians, did so. Among them, 11.3 million resided in Soviet Ukraine. Is this because borders kept changing? No, it is because people moved across what in the Soviet era were internal borders defining constituent national republics of the Union of Soviet Socialist Republics (USSR). Russians were not the only ones. In 1989, for instance, half a million Armenians lived in the Russian republic, as did 4.3 million Ukrainians (Itogi perepisi 2001 goda na Ukraine, 2003).

This Element explains the historical conditions for the seemingly anomalous presence of people outside of "their own" Soviet republic and the sometimes fraught consequences for them and their post-Soviet host countries. It does so with the understanding that the Soviet Union was "a state of nations" on the move. Planned and unplanned, forced and voluntary, temporary and permanent, relocations animated the broad political geography of the USSR (see Figure 2). A central feature of the Soviet Union was the imperious assignment of nationality to every part of the country and every individual, as inscribed in citizens' internal passports. National units formed an administrative hierarchy from Union republics to autonomous republics, oblasts, *krais*, and even, for a short while, districts. Nearly every geographical space carried a national character, each with corresponding titular linguistic and cultural attributes (Suny and Martin, 2001: 3–20).

Because in the Soviet Union each individual bore a national identity, transnational migration meant the creation of internal diasporas. By diasporas we mean groups identifiable by nationality living outside their designated "home" territory within the USSR. Moving across national boundaries was a nearly constant feature of Soviet history, which accounts for the expansion and contraction of diasporas. Returning to one's putative homeland or remaining outside of it depended on a multitude of factors. In what follows, we principally concern ourselves with the legal category of nationality rather than ethnic ties and rely on several decades of historical scholarship emphasizing how nationality was constructed in the context of Soviet imperial rule. Our understanding

Figure 1 Number of Russians outside borders of Russia in millions

of migration within Soviet space thus aligns with that of Erik Scott, for whom it "was an empire of mobile diasporas that transcended the borders of the republics" (Scott, 2016: 3).

We analyze these processes as functions of what we call regimes and repertoires of migration. We have defined regimes of migration as the "policies, practices, and infrastructure designed to both foster and limit human movement" (Siegelbaum and Moch, 2014: 3). They loomed large in the Soviet Union, essential to the Soviet state's big projects – the collectivization of agriculture and rapid industrialization, preemptive and retributive deportations, wartime mobilization and evacuation, and opening virgin land to cultivation and other developmental programs. All such undertakings involved moving people – millions of people – sometimes great distances and often across internal national boundaries. During a twenty-year period, from the beginning of the 1930s until the early 1950s, nationality figured centrally in Soviet migration regimes. Some of those regimes entailed selectively purging certain "elements" from the national body deemed dangerous or guilty of past infractions. In other cases, the objective was the relocation of an entire national group and the obliteration of its homeland from the map. But even when the state did not seek to relocate citizens of a particular nationality, the national distribution of the population was almost invariably altered. All these instances contributed to the making of diasporas.

Migrants' own repertoires – "their relationships and networks of contact that permitted adaptation to particular migration regimes" – could coincide with and

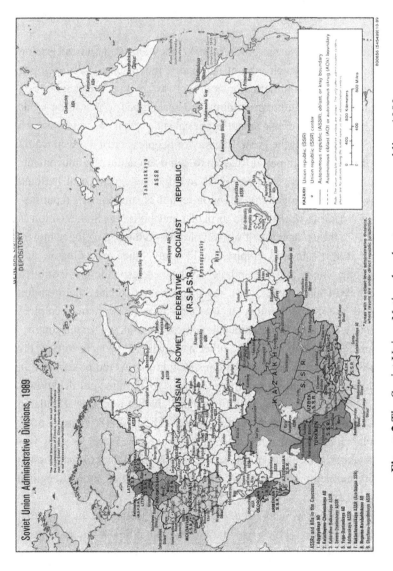

Figure 2 The Soviet Union: National and autonomous republics, 1989

reinforce regimes but also mitigate their harsh effects and even sabotage them (Siegelbaum and Moch, 2014: 5). The sort of thing that crops up in our study is when potential recruits signed up or didn't, or when a migrant reported back to friends or relatives about conditions in the diaspora, encouraging them to join or to stay away. To include repertoires is to recognize that migrants are social beings with ties of friendship and family to consider and that their dispositions and reactions matter.

When the Bolsheviks seized power in 1917, they did so in a disintegrating multiethnic empire in which vibrant nationalist movements had developed along its western and southern borders. Well aware that the neighboring Austro-Hungarian and Ottoman empires had succumbed to just these kinds of forces, they set out to create an anti-imperial state of nations, one in which the institutionalization of the great diversity of peoples across Eurasia would overcome the legacy of Imperial Russian rule and sap nationalist movements of their energy. They did, however, acknowledge the existence of national differences – hence the hierarchy of Union republics, autonomous republics, autonomous territories (*krai*), and so forth that they built. The Soviet Union as it emerged from the devastation of war-revolution-civil war developed into an empire, but it was "an odd empire," unlike any other preceding it, and migration both within and beyond its borders correspondingly exhibited distinct features (Suny, 1993: 128). As one very influential interpretation characterized the Soviet Union, it was an "affirmative action empire" (Martin, 2001). Russians occupied a paradoxical position within the country. On one hand, far outnumbering any other nationality, they were to play the leading role in the drama of socialist construction that would be narrated in Russian, the inevitable choice as a lingua franca. On the other, political power lay not in specifically Russian institutions, which in fact were less articulated in the Russian Soviet *Federated* Socialist Republic (RSFSR) than in other union republics, but rather in the All-Union Communist Party. Moscow was the *Party's* center, the capital of the Soviet empire more than of the Russian republic, its multiethnicity serving as a symbol of Soviet internationalism (Scott, 2016: 12).

It would be unwise to ignore the importance of ideology in the ways that Soviet citizens understood their own nationality within Soviet imperial space. Notions of "Soviet internationalism" and "the friendship of the peoples" as well as the endlessly repeated formula of "national in form, socialist in content" permeated Soviet discourse. Especially with the encouragement of Nikita Khrushchev in the late 1950s and early 1960s, ideologists envisioned the creation of a single Soviet people through the progressive drawing together (*sblizhenie*) and eventual merging (*sliianie*) of nations. This supranational

Soviet civic identity, though projected into the undefined future, overlay constituent national belonging. Perhaps its most impressive and intimate manifestation in everyday life was intermarriage.

The strength of a Soviet identity waned over time, although it did not disappear even with the fall of the Soviet Union in 1991. The transition to fifteen independent post-Soviet nation-states, accompanied by an upsurge in political nationalism, was indeed a messy and protracted process. Rates of migration increased exponentially as economies buckled and political strife – often interethnic – spread. Changes in the status of borders rendered international what had been internal migrations. Moreover, some emigrants traveled farther afield, seeking to take advantage of the new globalized economy. Likewise, people from distant corners of the world appeared in unprecedented numbers on the streets of major post-Soviet cities. Diasporas thus were made and unmade but also did not disappear.

We begin our inquiry into how Soviet patterns of migration shaped the post-Soviet landscape with an analysis of the most massive displacements of the Stalin era – nationality-based deportations. We proceed from the punitive wartime deportations in the Caucasus, comparing them with the removals of borderland and diasporic peoples dating from the early 1930s to the early 1950s. In contrast to the Caucasian deportations, these, motivated largely by security concerns, were selective, bearing similarities to the dekulakization drive associated with the collectivization of agriculture. Nevertheless, we argue, all deportations bore certain similarities and, in some respects, resembled other massive operations such as evacuation and even supposedly voluntary resettlement of lands vacated by deportees. Section 1 concludes with several examples of the life trajectories of deportees' children as they moved transnationally within the Soviet Union and in the process developed supranational, Soviet (and post-Soviet) "international(ist)" identities.

After a brief survey of urban diasporas in Central Asia and the Caucasus, Section 2 visits disparate parts of the country – from Donbas to Magnitogorsk to the Baltic republics, the cotton fields of Azerbaijan, thinly populated steppe land in Siberia and Sakhalin Island, the Virgin Lands of northern Kazakhstan, and eventually, Moscow and Leningrad – that served as magnets attracting Soviet citizens from throughout the country. These sites reflected regimes of labor and career migration intended to match population with areas rich in natural resources but also figured in migrants' repertoires of expanding income by engaging in the burgeoning shadow economy. All these cases of voluntary migration contrast with those featured in Section 1, which emphasized coercion. Even as diasporas formed in these places, we argue, they were instrumental in shaping the "new Soviet individual."

Section 3 is devoted to the history of immigration and emigration. Political sympathies as well as economic motivations could inspire people to move to the Soviet Union, but how their immigration relates to the theme of diaspora depends on whether they settled in a preexisting, officially designated national territory, or remained distinct amidst their Soviet hosts. To wit, whereas American technical personnel and Spanish refugee children were conspicuous as nationally defined communities, Armenian immigrants and Russians from China blended in with their conationals, albeit uneasily. If the former groups made diasporas, the latter engaged in unmaking them. We also address an in-between group – North American Finns who settled in Karelia bordering on independent Finland.

We analyze emigration from the Soviet Union in terms of four "waves": the White emigration following the October Revolution and civil war, those who remained abroad after the force majeure separations of the Second World War, Cold War–induced refugees and defectors, and those taking advantage of their "home" countries' right-of-return policies. In terms of nationality, when Russians and Ukrainians emigrated from the Soviet Union, they formed dia-sporic communities worldwide – in South and North America, Europe, and Asia, as well as in Australia. Other emigrants, such as Soviet Germans and Greeks, departed for their national homelands; however, many generations (or indeed centuries) had passed since their ancestors had left. Jews, the classic diasporic people, pursued both repertoires. Israel, the titular homeland of the Jewish people, absorbed many Soviet Jews from the 1960s onward. But Soviet Jews also formed or joined diasporas elsewhere in the world.

Up to the end of the Soviet Union, immigration and emigration are relatively easy to distinguish. Immigrants, for our purposes, refers to those who arrived in the USSR from abroad whereas emigrants left the USSR to live elsewhere. But with the formation of fifteen new independent post-Soviet states things get complicated. A Russian woman from Karaganda, Kazakhstan, who moves to, say, the Russian city of Samara simultaneously emigrates from one former Soviet republic and settles in – that is, immigrates to – another. In which context should we discuss her? We have decided to combine analyses of emigration and immigration. We consider post-Soviet immigration as part of the process of national consolidations that began before the Soviet Union broke up, but from the perspective of emigration, it meant the unmaking of national diasporas (Brubaker, 1995). We recognize economic inequalities among the successor states as having stimulated departures from the relatively poor ones and arrivals where conditions had become more robust or promising. The rapid transform-ation of Moscow into a global city attracting cheap sources of labor from the former Soviet republics and beyond receives special attention as does the multifarious phenomenon known as human trafficking and the officially sponsored efforts in the Russian Federation to attract "compatriots" from abroad.

Our consideration of the making of national diasporas in the Soviet Union and the effects of this kind of migration beyond 1991 terminates with the war in Ukraine that began in 2014 and took on massive dimensions with the full-scale Russian invasion of that country in February 2022. One of the lamentable consequences of this war has been the displacement of large numbers of Ukrainian women, children, and elderly persons seeking safety elsewhere in the country or abroad, primarily in Central and Eastern Europe, but also in Russia. We end with Russians, mostly male and of draft age, fleeing across their country's borders to Georgia, Kyrgyzstan, and other successor states.

Migration is an unwieldy subject. We have not sought to include every group of migrants who entered, moved within, or left the territories of the USSR – a truly gargantuan task. Rather, we aim to establish a comprehensive though still intelligible overview of patterns of migration as they have shaped and were shaped by the political, economic, and cultural forces in the different Soviet republics and the post-Soviet states. We do feel strongly about including the voices and stories of individual migrants, not only as illustrative tales but to engage with their perspectives on changing places and, often, identities. We devote special attention to non-Russians both as part of distinct national communities and as individual actors frequently making life-changing decisions. We thereby hope to contribute not only to the decolonization of Russian and Soviet history but also to the "de-essentialization" of national histories.

1 National Deportations and Diffusions

In the middle of May 1944, within the brief span of seventy-two hours, servicemen from the People's Commissariat for Internal Affairs (Naródnyi komissariát vnútrennikh del) (NKVD) rounded up for deportation the entire Tatar population in Crimea, then an Autonomous Soviet Socialist Republic (ASSR) within the RSFSR. Some 47,000 Crimean Tatar families, descendants of various Turkic-speaking, Muslim ethnic groups that had inhabited this salubrious peninsula for centuries, lost not only their homes but also their homeland. How was it possible to execute this operation with such appalling efficiency? The simple answer is that the NKVD had a lot of practice. National deportations, small-scale and rare before the 1930s, became more frequent and massive with the growing prospect of European war and then its reality. The Crimean Tatars were the sixth and almost the last national group in the Soviet Union to undergo forcible and complete expulsion.

The legal basis for these actions consisted of decrees issued by central bodies of the Soviet state. In October 1943, the Supreme Soviet decreed that "due to the fact that during the period of occupation of the Karachai Autonomous Oblast by the German fascist aggressors many Karachais behaved traitorously ... all Karachais residing on the territory" located in the North Caucasus would be banished "to other regions" of the country. The decree also liquidated the Karachai Autonomous Oblast. The next month, a similar decree applied to the Kalmyks (and their autonomous oblast of the lower Volga) "many" of whom "had betrayed the Motherland." In February–March 1944, it was the turn of the Balkars, the Chechens, and the Ingush, all peoples of the North Caucasus. Two months later, the State Defense Committee drafted a decree signed by Josef Stalin mandating the removal of the Crimean Tatars (Pobol' and Polian, 2005: 393, 412, 458, 489, 497).

Given the severity of their punishment, one might wonder whether these national groups had engaged in traitorous behavior to an extraordinary degree. The record suggests nothing of the sort. Many Ukrainians and Russians had lived under Nazi German occupation too, and some who ardently collaborated with the enemy paid for it dearly after liberation. But Russians and Ukrainians were too numerous to deport as a whole. With a total population of 134,402 in 1939, the Kalmyks were moveable. No less so the Karachais, who numbered 75,737, and the Balkars with 42,600 individuals. Aside from this "small peoples" thesis, historians have put forward other possible motives. One, particularly appropriate to the Chechens and Ingush, had to do with the historical unruliness of the region as indicated by low rates of military recruitment and high rates of desertion. Deportation and dispersion, according to this scenario, would facilitate sovietization (Zemskov, 2003: 107). Last, and with particular reference to the Crimean Tatars, Soviet expectations of conflict with Turkey after victory in Europe raised concern over ethnic affinities.

The swiftness of these operations is particularly impressive in the case of the largest one – the uprooting of nearly 500,000 Chechens and Ingush. The NKVD deployed more than 100,000 troops, the majority of whom already had accumulated similar experience. It took them a week to accomplish their task, meeting resistance with brutality that included slaughtering whole communities and executing arbitrarily children and the elderly (Pobol' and Polian, 2005: 436–42, 473). The surviving deportees boarded boxcars (in Russian, *teplushki*) equipped with stoves and bunks for the journey east. This method of large-scale human transport had many uses throughout Russia's twentieth century. *Teplushki* carried soldiers, settlers, evacuees, and deportees typically not in comfort but in close quarters. They served as wheeled homes for all six of the deported nations for weeks if not months.

Where did these convoys go? They went far away because Soviet authorities, in Judith Pallot and Laura Piacentini's terms, used "geography as punishment" (Pallot and Piacentini, 2012: 293). Most deposited their human cargo in Kazakhstan, which, in the span of some fifteen years already had become home to a variety of migrant groups, most of them involuntary. But having absorbed most of the Ingush and Chechens, Kazakhstan evidently reached its point of saturation. When it became the Crimean Tatars' turn, the Uzbek SSR beckoned, with the Urals and Siberia serving as secondary destinations.

Like earlier groups of deportees, the national groups we are discussing here bore the official designation of "special settlers," and their destinations were called "special settlements." Typically established in previously uninhabited areas with rudimentary housing and few other amenities, the special settlements constituted a major institution within the Soviet state's carceral regime. It embraced even those who had served honorably in the Red Army if they belonged to one of the condemned nationalities. Having initially assumed that deportation applied only to collaborators, the honorably discharged Server Akimov, a Crimean Tatar, not only found his family among the special settlers in Uzbekistan but also discovered that he too had to register once a month with the local commandant (Akimov, 2009). Alim Bekirov, another Crimean Tatar soldier, recalls reacting with indignation upon learning of his new status. "Nobody resettled me … I came from the army – here are my papers!" he exclaimed (Bekirov, 2009).

Special (also known as labor) settlements originated in connection with collectivization, or rather, dekulakization. With a nod to Alexander Solzhenitsyn's sobriquet for the labor camps, Lynne Viola referred to them as "the other archipelago," scattered as they were throughout remote regions of the Northern Territory, the Urals, western and eastern Siberia, and Kazakhstan (Viola, 2001: 730–55). They eventually accommodated deportees from a broad array of social categories – urban "social aliens," criminal recidivists and bandits, "pernicious" religious sects, and other marginal groups – all obviously in need of heavier doses of sovietization in the form of isolation and varying degrees of forced labor.

Here, we focus on the various borderland and diaspora "enemy nations" that Soviet authorities considered security risks so long as they remained in situ. Already in March 1930, the Politburo of the Communist Party's central committee ordered the deportation of some 13,000–18,500 "kulak families in the first instance of Polish nationality" from Belarusian and Ukrainian border regions, thereby "ethnicizing" one of its most proscribed categories (Brown, 2003: 83, 95–102; Pobol' and Polian, 2005: 41–2). Tensions heightened by Hitler's rise to power in Germany and Japan's absorption of Manchuria exacerbated what Terry Martin called "Soviet xenophobia," leading to large-scale ethnic cleansing of border regions. These began in 1935 and continued on and off for nearly three years. They resulted in the relocation of between a third and a half of all those identified as of Finnish, Polish, and German nationality. Particularly vulnerable were independent farming families living in special security zones originally defined as 22 kilometers from the border but eventually extending up to 100 kilometers. The removal of Koreans from the RSFSR's Far Eastern borders followed in 1937, with smaller-scale operations targeting ethnically "unreliable" elements – for example, Kurds, Iranians, Chinese – capping the process (Martin, 2001: 328–35).

The NKVD memoranda that prescribed procedures for deporting these groups bear striking similarities. Assisted by Party and Komsomol activists, regional NKVD personnel would select families, avoiding those with former Red partisans, Red Army soldiers, and reservists. Chosen families had to have resources – at least one able-bodied member, a two-month supply of food, and sufficient clothes and footwear. The memoranda deemed appropriate for every five families a horse – and "if possible," a cow – and each could bring about seventy pounds of domestic necessities and all the money they had. The convoys in which they traveled would each include two cars for food preparation. To ensure that the families would cooperate, heads of households would be taken into custody before departure (Danilov, Manning, and Viola, 1999–2006: 4:510, 530–1; Zemskov, 2003: 78).

Thus supplied, these deportees – kulaks of a national flavor – ideally could survive deep within the interior. However, at least one official, in charge of deportations from the Marchlevsk Polish Autonomous Region of western Ukraine, expressed shock at how little reality matched the program on paper. Nonetheless, off they went, some to the White Sea–Baltic Canal, site of one of the major construction projects of the First Five-Year Plan that relied primarily on Gulag labor, others to the Siberian taiga (Krasnoiarsk krai), while still others made it to southwestern Tajikistan's Vakhsh valley. Kate Brown notes in reference to the Polish deportees that never had their national identity mattered more than in exile (Brown, 2003: 136–49). This observation holds for virtually all other national minorities that made such journeys.

The search for security created additional insecurities. The acquisition of territories in the west stemming from the nonaggression pact with Germany occasioned a whole new round of nationality-based deportations. Selecting who among the 22 million new Soviet citizens should be deported eastward could not have been easy. Class certainly played a role in determining who might have had "a compromised social and political past," but it was only one factor among many. In the course of 1940, 211 convoys transported three different groups of former citizens of Poland amounting to some 270,000 individuals: army veterans and their families to whom the Polish government had granted homesteads in the eastern Polish provinces (*osadniki* in Russian; *osadnicy* in Polish); an eclectic group of registered prostitutes as well as family members of Polish officers executed by the NKVD at Katyn; and refugees from Poland's western provinces who refused Soviet citizenship and were overwhelmingly Jewish (Gur'ianov, 1997: 114–16).

Dispatched to 563 special settlements in the Russian north and Siberia, the *osadniki* received an amnesty and their liberation after the Nazi invasion of Soviet territory in June 1941. As many as 10,000 volunteered for the Polish armed forces in the east – known as Anders' Army – and, granted passage with their families through Iran, linked up with the British in Palestine. The majority, however, stayed in the country, receiving Soviet passports and the right to live anywhere except in border regions and specially designated "regime" cities such as Moscow and Leningrad. Meanwhile, those from the other two categories of Polish deportees had quite different fates. Special settlements accommodated many, but so did prisons and labor camps, with substantial numbers of people moving from one to the other as labor needs dictated. Jews sent eastward to any of these carceral institutions undoubtedly considered themselves unfortunate, but the move most likely saved their lives, for it put them beyond the reach of the Nazis (Zemskov, 2003: 86; Polian, 2004: 119; Pobol' and Polian, 2005: 107–30).

As dizzying and eclectic as these displacements might appear, the search for borderland security involved yet three more major operations before the Nazi invasion. The NKVD scattered throughout several Siberian territories some 30,000 Ukrainian nationalists who had resisted Soviet rule. The three Baltic republics coughed up former officers, large landowners, businessmen, and other "unreliable elements" deemed likely to resist their transformation into Soviet republics, as did the Moldavian SSR, previously the eastern Romanian provinces of Bessarabia and Bukovina. Generally, the NKVD imprisoned male heads of households in camps and sent other family members to settlements in Siberia as "exiled settlers." That is how some 7,500 Lithuanians came to live in the Altai, 6,000 Latvians were settled in Krasnoiarsk krai, and more than 11,000 Moldavians moved to Novosibirsk and Omsk oblasts (Zemskov, 2003: 91; Pobol' and Polian, 2005: 259).

The largest group of nationality-based deportees consisted of Soviet Germans. Of the 1.4 million counted in the 1939 census, slightly more than a million were sent to special settlements in Kazakhstan and Siberia. Nearly half came from the Volga German Autonomous Republic, which had originated as a "workers' commune" in October 1918 on the basis of German settlements originating in the eighteenth century. "Carts, carts, carts in front and behind as far as the eye could see," recalled one of them, Evgenii Miller, who was ten when he and his family traveled to the Volga whence they boarded barges for the long journey that ended in the Altai (Berdinskikh, 2005: 464–5). Berta Bachmann, arriving from Ukraine with her mother and two brothers at their lodgings (a "low-beamed mud hut") in Kazakhstan, wondered, "Is it possible that people live like this, like cattle in a stall?" (Bachmann, 1983: 20).

Up to that point, some forced to abandon their homes couldn't be sure whether they were being sent eastward for their own protection or had become interned as a potential fifth columnist. The authorities themselves tended to use the term "evacuation," and, at least in Kazakhstan, personnel assigned to assist evacuees treated the German "settlers" no differently than the others. Uniquely among the national deportees, though, able-bodied Soviet Germans had to serve in militarized labor formations known as labor armies. Recruits cut timber, constructed factories and railroads, and mined coal (German and Kurochkin, 1998: 136–42; Berdinskikh, 2005: 466–70). Their situation and treatment thus bore striking similarities to what Japanese internees experienced contemporaneously in North America.

Before proceeding to additional deportations that occurred late in the war and in the immediate postwar years, we need to briefly address another form of wartime impressment. The mass mobilization of Central Asians – Uzbeks, Tajiks, and Kazakhs – comes closest to the labor armies consisting of German deportees. After several months of fitful attempts to send ill-prepared workers to labor-starved industrial enterprises in the Urals and western Siberia, a committee under the USSR Council of Peoples Commissars directed the Commissariat of Defense in October 1942 to recruit 350,000 collective farmers from the region. Overwhelmingly if not exclusively male, they had to be between the ages of nineteen and fifty and deemed fit for unskilled, physically demanding work even if unfit for military service. Wartime shortages of bedding, food, and equipment plagued the recruits, as did their unfamiliarity with industrial work and ill treatment by mainly Russian managers. In some places, improvements occurred after workers petitioned and Party officials intervened, but the program itself became increasingly intolerable as victory in the war was in sight. In August 1944, Party and government leaders in Kazakhstan unprecedentedly appealed to the State Defense Committee to order the recall of all Kazakh workers, but not until May 1946 did the program end (Goldman, 2022).

By then, the leadership of the Georgian SSR had succeeded in ridding the republic of the "Turkish Muslim" minorities, thereby helping to consolidate the rule of the titular nationals. It didn't hurt this effort that the two most powerful people in the country – Stalin and his NKVD chief, Lavrenty Beria, hailed from Georgia (Kaiser, 2019: 82–3). The operations recall prewar border clearances of ethnic groups considered unreliable, but now along the southern border with Turkey. In November 1944, the NKVD uprooted the entire population of Meskhetian Turks as well as Kurds, and "Khemshils" (Sunni Muslim Armenians) residing in southern Georgia. Some 91,000 people went into exile, more than half to Uzbekistan and the remainder to Kazakhstan and Kyrgyzstan. The Meskhetian Turks joined the five other Muslim peoples of the Caucasus in the totality of their deportation and elimination of their nationally designated homeland. They also belong with Crimean Tatars and Volga Germans to an unenviable trio denied the right of return for decades to come, one of the "loose ends," as British novelist Penelope Lively describes the other two, that did not rise to the level of "perennial matters for international reproach" (Lively, 1987: 134; Bugai and Gonov, 1998: 214–15).

The reverberations of the Cold War would follow deportees deep into the interior of the country. When in 1945, Beria ordered the construction of a secret facility in the Urals to produce plutonium, German internees provided much of the labor. But by 1951, with the closed city of Ozersk up and running, General Ivan Tkachenko, the NKVD official in charge, promised to "banish all the Germans from our city." While some with highly valued skills avoided this additional deportation, thousands were removed, including two doctors who wound up in Kolyma, among the most remote and harshest of camps in the Gulag system. The stringency of the security zone also excluded Tatars and Bashkirs, who made up most of the region's population. As Kate Brown writes, "Tkachenko and his staff interpreted loyalty and trustworthiness in national terms – as largely Russian and sometimes Ukrainian" (Brown, 2013: 89, 110, 157).

In a reprise of 1941, western Ukraine, the Baltics, and Moldavia furnished new candidates for deportation after the end of the Great Patriotic War. This time, the pool was more democratic, including those who allegedly had taken up arms against the Red Army – for example, as members of the Ukrainian Insurgent Army or the guerrilla bands known in the Baltics as the Forest Brothers – as well as "kulaks … and activists of pro-fascist parties" in the case of Moldavia. Additionally, those identified as belonging to groups of questionable loyalty to the Soviet Union because of their perceived sympathies with bordering states outside the sphere of Soviet domination or with a history of unauthorized nationalism found themselves expelled. Their forced migrations from 1947 to 1952 proceeded as a series of evocatively code-named operations of the successor to the NKVD, the Ministry of State Security (Ministerstvo gosudarstvennoi bczopasnosti) (MGB):

- Operation West/Zapad (August 1947) – deported approximately 26,000 families containing 78,000 individuals from western Ukraine to Kazakhstan and western Siberia (Zemskov, 2003: 198, 210; Pobol' and Polian, 2005: 568, 576, 579).

- Operation Springtime/Vesna (May 1948) – deported some 50,000 Lithuanians suspected of being anti-Soviet partisans, opponents of collectivization, and their families to Krasnoiarsk Krai, Irkutsk Oblast, and the Buryat-Mongol ASSR (Bugai, 1995: 210).
- Operation Surf/Priboi (January–March 1949) – deported 87,000 Estonians, Latvians, and Lithuanians suspected of being kulaks, bandits, nationalists, and members of their families, to inhospitable locations in Siberia and the Far North (Bugai, 1995: 229).
- Operation Wave/Volna (May–June 1949) – deported more than 57,000 diasporic Greeks and Turks as well as Dashnaks (Armenians accused of nationalist activism inspired by the pre-1917 movement, the Armenian Revolutionary Federation) from mainly the Georgian and Armenian SSRs to Kazakhstan and Siberia (Kaiser, 2019: 80–94).
- Operation North/Sever (April 1951) – targeted Jehovah's Witnesses in the western Soviet republics (Ukraine, Moldavia, Belarus), numbering nearly 10,000, for deportation to Tomsk and Irkutsk oblasts in Siberia (King, 2000: 96; Polian, 2004: 333).

From the many accounts of what deportees endured we select Aili Valdrand's. In 1949, five years after her father had fled to Sweden to avoid falling into the hands of "the Russians," Aili, a thirteen-year-old Estonian, accompanied her kulak mother into internal exile. They followed the path blazed by earlier Estonian deportees, some 1,619 of whom had been resettled in Novosibirsk oblast. Aili's new home away from home was a dairy farm located near the town of Tatarsk in the western part of the oblast, not far from the border with Kazakhstan (Kirss and Hinrikus, 2009: 439–55).

Aili Valdrand was one of 26,305 children and her mother one of 40,877 women deported from the Baltic region as of 1949. Women and children in fact outnumbered men, not only among Estonians or Baltic peoples but in every category of national deportees. Of the nearly 2.1 million people in this category by July 1949, women made up 38 percent, children 36 percent, and men only 26 percent (Zemskov, 2003: 167). Why was this so? It was probably because of the gendered skewing of wartime and postwar civilian populations due to military recruitment and the determination of the NKVD to round up and resettle entire families, but also because husbands, fathers, and other men disproportionately populated the Gulag.

The story is similar for the Ingrian Finns whose misfortune was to inhabit territory too close to Leningrad for the comfort of Stalin's security-conscious agents. Those not expelled to the interior (Central Asia and Siberia) in 1935 and 1936 experienced the Winter War of 1939–40 at close hand, with many families fleeing westward to Finland. After the Nazis invaded the Soviet Union and blockaded Leningrad, Ingrians living in the Karelian isthmus and along the southern coast of the Gulf of Finland found themselves in German-held territory while the some 20,000 who inhabited lands to the north and east of the city were deported by the NKVD to Siberia in early 1942.

During 1943–4, the Germans and the Finnish government arranged for the evacuation of the Ingrians to Finland, but most – some 55,000 – returned to Soviet jurisdiction later in 1944 in accordance with Point 10 of the Moscow Armistice, which ended the so-called Continuation War. They could not reoccupy their former homes, however, because Soviet authorities had reserved them for presumably more reliable Russian settlers. Most entrained for those repositories of forced resettlement – Siberia's Krasnoiarsk krai and Irkutsk oblast (Matley, 1979: 10–16; Zemskov, 2003: 95). Like Aili Valdrand and other Baltic deportees, Ingrians were permitted to leave their places of exile after 1956. Some settled in the Finnic-speaking Estonian SSR and Karelian ASSR. Those choosing to stay adapted to life in Siberia, essentially Russifying themselves.

Deported peoples, in the words of successive decrees from the period, were to be "permanently evicted." A substantial number, though, refused to abide and escaped. Between 1941 and 1946, they totaled more than 57,000, of whom only 13 percent (7,686 individuals) were apprehended. Whether they found cover back home or changed their identities and lived elsewhere is not clear. Eventually, the security organs caught up with most escapees: as of May 1953, a little more than 2,000 of the 87,745 who had escaped were still at large (Zemskov, 2003: 191).

Most deportees stayed in the special settlements until amnestied, though with special skills sometimes came special dispensation. Decrees from 1956–8 permitted those from the north Caucasus – the Kalmyks, Balkars, Karachai, Ingush, and Chechens – to return to their national homelands, which had had their status as autonomous oblasts restored. The same held for Greeks, Kurds, and Turks who returned to non-titular territories, namely as minorities within the Armenian and Georgian SSRs. However, returns were often bittersweet. In many cases, reclaiming homelands turned out to be easier than reclaiming homes. Conflicts, sometimes violent, occurred with settlers who had occupied deportees' homes in the interim. Infrastructure had deteriorated or been damaged. Relations with other north Caucasian peoples who had not been deported proved tense.

Elsewhere, returns could be complicated too. To illustrate, let us return to Aili Valdrand's story. She arrived back in Soviet Estonia in 1958 after a nine-year absence. Her Siberian sojourn, she notes, marked her in various ways. She observes, for example, that as the train moved westward, passengers demonstrated less friendliness. Having learned to speak fluent and unaccented Russian, she "felt stupid and backward" in Estonia. Her most significant relationship was with a fellow Siberian exile with whom she had a child. She couldn't make a decent living and had to rely on "scraps from other people's tables" to feed her son. People back home, she wrote in her memoir from the 1990s, "cannot understand us [Siberian exiles]." In 1989, when hostility toward the Soviet Union was exploding in the Baltic, Valdrand rescued Russian-language books the local daycare center had discarded (Kirss and Hinrikus, 2009: 453–5).

How different was the life story of returnee Dzhokhar Dudayev, born in February 1944, a few days before the deportation of Chechens to Kazakhstan. In 1957, he along with most Chechens returned home. After studying electronics, he entered the air force and joined the Communist Party in 1968. He pursued a Soviet military career that included stints in the Soviet-Afghan War and assignment as a major general in Tartu, Estonia. In 1990, however, he returned to Grozny, the Chechen capital, then convulsed by nationalist fervor. Dudayev took a leading role in the revolt in September 1991 to oust the Soviet government from Chechnya. As president of the newly independent Republic of Ichkeria, he led the successful resistance to Russian forces dispatched by Russian president Boris Yeltsin in the First Chechen War (1994–6). On April 21, 1996, this loyal son of Chechnya was assassinated by Russian operatives (Lieven, 1999: 58–64, 140).

Denied the right of return, other diasporic nations exhibited different itineraries. Meskhetian Turks largely stayed in Uzbekistan – until they couldn't. In June 1989, as Soviet internationalism (aka "friendship of the peoples") rapidly lost its purchase, clashes in the Fergana Valley between titular Uzbeks and Meskhetian Turks drove out most of the latter. Some emigrated to Turkey. Azerbaijan and Kazakhstan, also mainly Islamic and Turkic-speaking but additionally Soviet in terms of political and cultural heritage, took at least as many (Keller, 1989: 6; Meskhetian Turks).

Crimean Tatars received their right of return in 1989, after decades of unsuccessfully petitioning the Soviet government. Those who sought to reclaim their property, however, discovered that Russian and Ukrainian settlers had repopulated the peninsula, which Soviet leader Nikita Khrushchev had gifted to the Ukrainian SSR in 1954. But what of the lives of the exiled in the intervening decades? We turn to three Crimean Tatars during the late Soviet period and follow them beyond the Soviet Union's demise. Server Akimov joined his parents in Andizhan oblast, Uzbekistan, after his demobilization in 1946.

There, he pursued a career repairing oil wells. In 1956, freed from the obligation to stay in place, he left the Uzbek SSR for the Ukrainian SSR. For the next ten years, he worked on a collective farm and then moved to the southern Ukrainian city of Melitopol until retirement. In 1993, he moved back to Crimea with his wife, gave his daughter away in marriage, and became a grandfather. Friends from Melitopol urged him to return there, but he expressed happiness to be "in my homeland" (*na rodine*) (Akimov, 2009).

Rasmie Chelokhaeva was ten when that "awful moment" of deportation occurred. For the next six months, she survived with her siblings in an Uzbek orphanage until rescued by their mother, her father having been killed at the front. In 1954, she graduated from a teacher's college in Kokand, got a job teaching in a local school, and married a fellow deportee. She and her husband stayed in Uzbekistan for the next forty years. All the time, she told an interviewer, she wanted to return to Crimea, citing the proverb "Better to live like a pauper in your own land than like a tsar in a foreign land." In 1994, she and her husband realized this desire (Chelokhaeva, 2009).

When Server and Rasmie repatriated, ethnic Russians comprised some two-thirds of Crimea's population while Ukrainians made up about a quarter. Substantial numbers of deportees and their descendants returned during the 1990s, many (at least according to a 1998 survey) experiencing worse material conditions after their return. Census data from 2014 indicate some 240,000 (about 12 percent of the entire Crimean population) identify as Tatar (Itogi perepisi 2001 goda na Ukraine, 2003). The Russian government, which seized Crimea from Ukraine in that year, officially considers them a "national minority." As heartwarming as it may be to learn of Server and Rasmie's return, most deportees and their descendants followed other paths.

Fayziya Ablyakimova's story as related to Lewis in the late 1990s is suggestive of the available possibilities. Raised in Ashgabat, Turkmenistan's capital city, Fayziya met and married a fellow Crimean Tatar. Sometime in the 1970s, she and her husband took jobs in Fergana, Uzbekistan, she as an English teacher and he as a gym instructor. After 1989, moving to Crimea became an option, but they did not pursue it. Children of displaced parents, they pursued successful careers in a Central Asian republic different from the one in which they were raised. They thereby illustrate a widespread pattern of Soviet transnationalism and a Soviet identity that they seamlessly carried over into the post-Soviet years (Siegelbaum, 2019: 128–9).

Fayziya and her husband shared the city not only with Uzbeks, Tajiks, and Russians but also with a substantial community of Koreans, descendants of those deported from Russia's Far Eastern borders in 1937. Altogether, the

NKVD had sent about 100,000 Koreans to Kazakhstan, 70,000 to Uzbekistan, and smaller numbers to Turkmenistan, Kyrgyzstan, and the RSFSR. Those Lewis encountered in the late 1990s in a Fergana city park wore national costumes to perform Korean dances. They thereby evoked their national identity despite decades of separation from their Soviet border homeland. The cultivation of bok choy, onions, and rice on the kolkhozes and sovkhozes formed upon their arrival in Central Asia was another indication of the survival of their Korean ways. In the late 1960s, intrepid Koreans traveled on their own to the shores of the Black Sea in Soviet Ukraine to cultivate onions and proved so successful at it that Ukrainian brigades following their example became known as "Koreans" (Siegelbaum and Moch, 2016: 978–9; Kokaisl, 2018: 1–25).

During the Great Patriotic War, Soviet authorities permitted only a few Koreans to serve in the Red Army, although some had received medals for bravery. Most, like Soviet Germans, formed segregated labor armies that inter alia mined coal in Karaganda and cut timber in the northern Urals (Gelb, 1995: 406–7). After the war, Korean kolkhozes gained a reputation as "models of efficiency and prosperity" throughout Central Asia. In subsequent decades, as Koreans became more urbanized, they also became high achievers in other endeavors. They had a higher proportion of "Heroes of Socialist Labor" than any other Soviet national group, and their children were most likely to go on to higher education (Gelb, 1995: 408–12). Soviet Koreans who achieved widespread fame in the USSR include historian M. P. Kim (1906–94), balladeer Iulii Kim (1936–), and rock legend Viktor Tsoi (1962–90). The latter two were born of highly educated Korean fathers and Russian mothers, mixed marriages that both resulted from and encouraged a Soviet identity.

Mixed marriages steadily increased throughout the country, rising from one in ten marriages in the 1950s to nearly one in seven according to 1989 census data. In a hotbed of newly arrived nationalities like Kazakhstan, rates of intermarriage were higher, rising from 14 percent in 1959 to 24 percent in 1979 (Susokolov, 1987: 142; Edgar, 2022). To be sure, most occurred between people of like groups – Russian and Belarusian or Ukrainian; Uzbek and Kirgiz or Turkmen. Still, when, during the 1970s, Saodat-opa, a Tajik woman, married Ilkhom-aka, an Uzbek she had met in the Komsomol, their respective families celebrated the wedding "as a sign of progressiveness," symbolizing the gathering strength of Soviet "internationalism" (Reeves, 2007: 280–2). Symbolizing the Cold War, international marriages involving Soviet citizens and foreigners were banned outright in 1947 and remained rare even after the lifting of the ban under Khrushchev.

2 Recruitment, Attractions, and New Beginnings

Deportations and evacuation created enormous diasporas in much of Central Asia and Siberia. But diasporic Russian and other European populations already existed in these parts of the country before the war years, indeed even before the 1917 Revolution. Before we analyze the grand projects that recruited rather than compelled people to migrate beyond regional and national borders, we survey these anterior diasporic communities and their expansion during the Great Patriotic War due to evacuation. We then turn to sites of industrialization – the Donbas region of Ukraine; Magnitogorsk located, as the memoir by an American who participated in this most emblematic of prewar Five-Year Plan construction projects had it, "behind the Urals"; Noril'sk in the Far North, initially dependent on forced labor but eventually resorting to incentives; and other even more far-flung spots. This is followed by analyses of the postwar resettlement of Slavic-speaking Soviet citizens in areas annexed in the course of the Great Patriotic War, efforts to establish a Soviet homeland for Jews in the Russian Far East, agricultural resettlement projects ranging from Azerbaijan to Kazakhstan and Central Russia, and, finally, migration from Central Asian and Caucasian cities to Moscow and Leningrad for education, professional training, and commerce. All such migrations in contrast to those discussed in Section 1 emanated at least to some degree from migrants' willingness to uproot themselves and try out a new place.

In 1959, nearly three-quarters of the residents of Alma-Ata, a city of more than 450,000 people and the capital of Kazakhstan, identified as Russian. Kazakhs comprised a mere 8.6 percent (Vsesoiuznaia perepis', 1959). Alma-Ata was only one of many major cities in Central Asia with a substantial Russian presence. How did it get that way? In 1854, as Russian rule expanded over the great Siberian steppe, a detachment of the Imperial Army established an outpost called Verny that within a year began to attract Russian settlers from Siberia and the southern Urals. It also would accommodate Cossacks who set up two *stanitsy* (villages) and a Tatar *slobodka* (settlement). The empire-wide census of 1897 revealed that nearly 22,800 people lived in Verny, 63.8 percent of whom were Russian and Ukrainian (Little Russian) speakers. Throughout Semirechye oblast, corresponding to northern Kazakhstan, such speakers amounted to less than 10 percent of the overall population of just under a million (Pervaia vseobshchaia perepis', 1905). In other words, the Russian presence in the future Kazakhstan was initially an urban one.

So it was elsewhere in Central Asia and the Caucasus. The stories of the founding of Bishkek (then called Pishpek and for much of the Soviet period Frunze), Kyrgyzstan, and Ashkhabad, Turkmenistan resemble that of Alma-Ata.

These were projections of Russian imperial rule, places where military garrisons and Cossack detachments ensured the security of administrators who followed. In the case of Kazakhstan, those administrators would themselves pave the way for rural settlers – more than 1.5 million between 1896 and 1916 – by overseeing the identification and surveying of lands from which the nomadic pastoralist peoples of the region would be barred (Cameron, 2018: 24–6). In the southern tier of the empire, Russians' presence can be explained by a different dynamic, that of natural resource exploitation. Baku, where oil became king, lured not only the Nobels' and Rothschilds' capital but also a Russian community that, by 1897, totaled 39,000, or slightly more than a third of the city's population (Pervaia vseobshchaia perepis', 1905).

The 1917 Revolution brought about the renunciation of colonial rule by the Bolsheviks, who established national republics, though initially not of equal status. From the early 1920s until 1936, for example, Kazakhstan was an autonomous republic within the RSFSR, while Azerbaijan resided within the Transcaucasian Socialist Federative Soviet Republic. Even afterward, though, one discovers that the proportions of Russians in the national capitals had increased. Alma-Ata's Russians constituted 72 percent of the population and Kazakhs only 11 percent in 1939. In Baku, Russians had upped their presence by the 1939 census to 43.5 percent, significantly greater not only than the Armenian community (15 percent) but also the titular Azerbaijani one, which amounted to 27.3 percent (Vsesoiuznaia perepis', 1959). However, what might appear as demographic continuity belies a profound shift in the nature of the Russian presence. Soviet infrastructural development meant educational, industrial, and administrative institutions that required trained personnel to run them, and those people came largely from European Russia. In the case of Tashkent, Uzbekistan's capital, the quantitative change was dramatic. If in 1897, Russian speakers were only 11 percent of the city's population, then by 1939, the community had mushroomed to 42.4 percent (Pervaia vseobshchaia perepis', 1905; Vsesoiuznaia perepis', 1959).

Then came the war and with it the evacuation of anywhere between 10 and 17 million Soviet citizens and about 20 percent of industrial enterprises from territory vulnerable to Nazi occupation, all sent eastward within the span of eighteen months. Overseen by the Council for Evacuation, a body created two days after the German invasion, the process inevitably involved arm-twisting, disorderliness, unintended family separations, and other mishaps (Manley, 2009: 267–8). Nobody could know the price of leaving or staying. Frequently, people made decisions on the spur of the moment. The point is that they had a degree of choice, unlike the deportees. The evacuees – Russians, Ukrainians, Belarusians, Jews, and trusted citizens of the Baltic region – would alter the balance of nationalities in their wartime refuges. Designated destinations generally did not depend on evacuees' nationality but rather on determinations of each region's capacity to absorb them, and other factors including evacuees' repertoires of migration. Some wound up in small towns where, as Abram Tseitlin, evacuated with his parents and siblings from Ukraine's Vinnitsa oblast to Kermine, Uzbekistan, recalled half a century later, "Everything was different – The language . . . the scorching sun, the mudbrick homes and outbuildings, the colorful market, the fruits I had never seen before, the Uzbeks." As it happened, the Tseitlins were not the only newcomers in Kermine. The town also hosted contingents of Polish *osadniki* who competed with Abram and his fellow Jewish evacuees in those colorful markets for goods in short supply. Trading of insults, he reports, included anti-Semitic taunts and even on one occasion a pogrom replete with "sticks, stones, and boards" (USHMM RG-31.053, Tseitlin, 1990).

Some inevitably had it better than others. For example, in October 1941, poet Anna Akhmatova flew (!) some 1,500 kilometers from besieged Leningrad to Chistopol in the Tatar ASSR. There, she met up with Lydia Chukovskaia, daughter of the famous children's author Kornei Chukovskii, who had arranged for them to join him in Tashkent. Lydia and her daughter had left Moscow aboard a steamer that took them along the Moscow–Volga canal and thence to Chistopol on the Kama River. Once Akhmatova announced she was joining them, they proceeded by train from Kazan, the Tatar republic's capital, along with other writers and their families. "I'm glad to be seeing so much of Russia," Akhmatova exclaimed as she gazed out of the window. Somewhere in Siberia, they passed a trainload of Volga German deportees also heading east and, after traversing mountains and desert, arrived in Tashkent (Chukovskaya, 1994: 184–93).

Tashkent accommodated other famous evacuees, among them composer Dimitri Shostakovich. It rivaled Alma-Ata, the Kazakh SSR capital, as the temporary home for the Soviet cultural elite. The luminaries would return to Moscow and Leningrad by war's end, but many evacuees remained and in succeeding years were joined by newcomers from European Russia. By 1959, Tashkent's Russian population had swelled to more than 400,000 (44 percent of the city's total) from less than 250,000 in 1939. Moreover, thanks primarily to evacuation, its European Jewish population had more than doubled from some 21,000 to 44,000. Elsewhere in Central Asia, Russians played an outsized role in urban development, supplying much of the cadres for industry, education, and administration. They dominated Frunze to the tune of 69 percent of its 1959 population and were half of Ashgabat's. In the Caucasus, Baku's Russians were more than a third (35 percent) of the population and its Armenians more than a fifth (21 percent), meaning these diasporic communities together constituted a majority. Neither Tbilisi nor Erevan supported a substantial Russian presence, though the proportion of Armenians in Georgia's capital resembled that of Baku. Not until the Soviet Union began to unravel in the late 1980s did these diasporic communities diminish (Vsesoiuznaia perepis', 1959).

Recent emphasis on the colonial nature of the Soviet Union as manifested most emblematically in Central Asia has tended to obscure the leading role of industrialization in the making of the Soviet Union and its ideological icon, "the new Soviet man." The country the Bolsheviks inherited from the tsars possessed few areas of industrial development. One, the Donets Basin (Donbas), had attracted Belgian, British, and French capital investment to develop its rich veins of coal, vital for steelmaking and other industrial processes. It also drew on a predominantly ethnic Russian labor force. Peasants from the central Russian provinces typically engaged in seasonal migration to the mines, returning home for planting and harvesting. Home, at least for some, gradually became the Donbas. This is how Nikita Khrushchev, born into a peasant family from Russia's Kursk province in 1894, wound up there. At fourteen, he joined his father in Iuzovka (from 1924 Stalino, and from 1961 Donetsk), apprenticing as a metal fitter and then repairing mining equipment in the nearby town of Rutchenkovo (Taubman, 2003: 26–38).

After the disruptions and destruction wrought by revolution and civil war, migration to the Donbas from Russia revived. The first All-Union Soviet census of 1926 thus recorded Russians as making up 56 percent of the Donbas's largest city, Stalino (as Iuzovka had just become known), whereas Ukrainians numbered 26 percent and Jews 11 percent (Stalino). As one historian wrote in the conclusion of his account of Iuzovka and revolution, "The Donbass ... remained within ... Ukraine but not of it" (Friedgut, 1989: 331). Nineteen twenty-seven marked the year Aleksei Stakhanov, who hailed from Russia's Orel province and would go on to become the most celebrated worker in the entire USSR, arrived at the Central Irmino mine in the Donbas. Within a few years, he would be joined by tens of thousands of peasants fleeing collectivization and seeking to survive as miners and other industrial workers in that part of Soviet Ukraine (Siegelbaum, 1988: 68–9).

In due course, the Donbas became one of those magnets that attracted demobilized soldiers, penurious collective farmers, and others from across the country willing to adapt to a strenuous industrial regimen. With Russian serving as the lingua franca, many people – not only in the Donbas but in other parts of Ukraine and Russia as well – abandoned their previous national identities or at least stopped caring much about them. If in the Soviet Union, nationality defined people, some people could define their nationality. The most famous example

Figure 3 Leonid Brezhnev's passport granted June 11, 1947

was future Soviet leader Leonid Ilych Brezhnev, born in Ekaterinoslav/ Katerinoslav'sk province in 1906 to migrants from Russia's Kursk province. In documents dating from 1942 and 1947 when he served first as a political commissar in the Red Army and then secretary of two central Ukrainian regional party organizations, his nationality is listed as Ukrainian, but others from 1943 and 1945 give it as Russian. It was all the same to Leonid Ilych ("Byl' ukraintsem, stal russkim. Kto byl' Brezhnev po natsional'nosti?" 2020) (see Figure 3).

For many, nationality had become subordinate to being Soviet. This mentality should not be confused with what historian Tara Zahra theorized in the context of Central Europe as "national indifference." As Brezhnev's biography suggests, declarations of nationality could be situational, designed to enhance career possibilities, for example. But it is important to remember that the Soviet state attached nationality to every citizen regardless of mentality or strategic considerations. By the late 1980s, that state showed clear signs of dissolution. For many in the Donbas, the prospect of an independent Ukraine did not evoke fear, for, thinking in strategic terms, they considered it possible to extract "a better deal" from Kyiv than they had been getting from Moscow. However, once Ukraine became an independent nation-state, those of Russian heritage found themselves in an awkward situation, like Donetsk resident Tatiana Samofalova, who in the summer of 1992, declared:

> I was born in Ukraine, and I've lived here all my life. My father, my husband's father, my grandparents are buried here. I believe that no one will expel me from Ukraine ... I have been converted into a Ukrainian to

such an extent that it's no problem for me to speak Ukrainian, though very few Russians do it. Even Ukrainians themselves forgot how to speak Ukrainian ... But it's not enough to live in independent Ukraine. My relatives, my aunt, my cousin, live in Russia and it has become a problem to go and see them. We cannot meet with each other very often, and letters don't get delivered. Why should I want such independence? What am I independent from? (Siegelbaum and Walkowitz, 1995: 117–22, 143–50, 197)

Tatiana's question has to do with the conversion of nominal internal Soviet borders into real international ones. It also presages the separatist revolt of 2014 in reaction to the ouster in Kyiv of President Yanukovych, a son of the Donbas. Suddenly, national heritage had become salient. Since the onset of fighting between the Ukrainian army and separatists backed by Russian forces, tens of thousands have left the Donbas, some westward into Ukraine and others in the opposite direction to Russia. Nationality evidently had come to matter a great deal more than had been the case decades earlier.

Donetsk owed its origin to Welshman John Hughes, who founded a steel mill in what he humbly called Iuzovka. By contrast, the premier city of Stalinist industrialization, Magnitogorsk, was of purely Soviet origin. It served as a magnet for people of more than forty nationalities. Some came out of a sense of excitement or ambition, their imaginations fired by visions of building the largest blast furnace in the world and, in the process, the New Soviet Man. Others arrived from fear of being labeled a kulak back in the village, or as special settlers, previously identified and punished as kulaks. One official assigned responsibility for preparing barracks for special settlers arranged for accommodations for 25,000 only to have 40,000 show up (Kotkin, 1993: 70–1).

Like other great worksites of the First -Five Year Plan (1928–32), only more so, Magnitogorsk was marked by a great churning turnover. "While breaking work records," writes Gabor Rittersporn, "the builders who left the legendary construction site of the Magnitogorsk steelworks amounted to twelve times the number of the yearly average contingent" of workers (Rittersporn, forthcoming). Departures were swift and voluminous. In 1931 alone, 116,703 people registered their departure. Ninety percent had spent less than six months in the city, many living in tents, and 50 percent stayed less than three months. These figures apply to only about a quarter of the number of people estimated to have actually left that year (Kotkin, 1993: 82–3).

Nevertheless, a sufficient number stayed long enough to build those blast furnaces as well as a city that accommodated some 250,000 people by the end of the decade. In the process, as Karl Schlögel recently has written, Magnitogorsk became a "workshop for manufacturing human beings," specifically, "a new

Soviet human being who regarded assimilation into the human fabric as more important than preserving national characteristics" (Schlögel, 2023: 107–8). In this respect, it performed the same function as the Donbas, Dneprostroi (the high dam built on the Dnipro River to improve shipping and provide additional electric power for the Donbas), the White Sea–Baltic Sea canal, and other major construction projects of the 1930s.

The weakening appeal of this ideology would in turn lead to the assertion or, depending on the nation, the reassertion of nationality. By that time, many of the heroic construction sites from the era of Soviet industrialization had lost their technological edge and the communities they had sustained ceased to be at the forefront of anything other than environmental degradation. When Karl Schlögel visited Magnitogorsk in 1992, shortly after it had opened to foreigners, he found himself speechless:

> I was aware of the statistics about the quantities of rust and poison gas raining down daily, weekly and annually . . . I knew that thousands upon thousands of poisonous particles were released into the air over the town when plumes of smoke of every conceivable color poured out of the chimneys over the industrial complex. I knew that Magnitogorsk ranked highest in every publication about air and water pollution, that the incidence of cancer was higher than elsewhere and that this was not a good place to bring babies into the world. (Schlögel, 2023: 142)

By 2007, when the New York-based Blacksmith Institute published its analysis of the most polluted places in the world, Magnitogorsk ranked among the "dirty thirty" (World's Worst Polluted Places, 2007). Among the top ten, four had Soviet pasts: Sumgait, Azerbaijan; Dzerzhinsk, Russia; Noril'sk, Russia; and Chernobyl, Ukraine. Sumgait, Azerbaijan's second most populous city and the site of a devastating pogrom against Armenians in 1988, gained notoriety again in 2007 when Blacksmith listed it as the world's most polluted city. But measures to clean up organic chemicals, oil, mercury, and other heavy metals have improved the local environment. Residues from chemicals production going back to the 1930s put Dzerzhinsk high on the list, and Chernobyl's woeful tale is well known. But Noril'sk, the northernmost city in the world, has its own story, and since it intersects with the dynamics of Soviet migration regimes, it requires elaboration here.

Founded in the 1930s as a far northern outpost of the Gulag, Noril'sk became increasingly dependent already in the 1940s on freely hired workers to mine its rich deposits of nickel, copper, and other metals. If in 1941, the ratio of prison to voluntary labor was 5:1, then by the end of that decade, it had dropped to 2:1. To be sure, most of the "volunteers" consisted of those confined to the camp even after the termination of their sentences. But a robust program to increase the proportion of truly voluntary laborers in such northern locales was already in the works. Known as the Northern Increment, it provided material incentives for working in inhospitable locations. The rewards included higher wages and salaries, longer vacation time, coverage of travel expenses, housing, and an accelerated pension schedule. In a continuing effort to lure people to develop the natural resources found in such far-flung areas, the state enhanced the system's emoluments several times in the 1950s and 1960s (Siegelbaum and Moch, 2014: 141–2).

Like Magadan, Vorkuta, and other former Gulag sites devoted to mineral extraction, Noril'sk expanded into a real city, its population rising from 13,886 in 1939 to 109,442 in 1959, and a peak of more than 180,000 in 1982. Thereafter, the "stagnation" that afflicted the entire country in the late Brezhnev-era years took its toll on Noril'sk. Departures began to outnumber arrivals such that by 1989, fewer than 175,000 lived in the city, and by 2005, fewer than 132,000. What remained was a mixture of those who had come via the Northern Increment and descendants of Gulag "zeks" (prisoners), a multinational population albeit 74 percent ethnic Russian. Some who departed returned to their previous homes (Natsional'nost' – noril'chane, 2020). For example, in 1989, a group of families fleeing Vorkuta explained to one of us during a flight to Donetsk they were "going home" because the Northern Increment could not compensate for the deprivation they were experiencing.

"Deprivation" was relative, of course, but health also suffered. The catastrophic decline of life expectancy throughout Russia in the 1990s continued in such locales as Vorkuta and Noril'sk primarily due to galloping pollution. The daily spewing of sulfur dioxide and other toxins led to elevated levels of respiratory diseases and cancer. As of 2010, life expectancy in the latter city was fifty-nine, ten years lower than the average in the rest of the Russian Federation (Fiore, 2017). Aside from the Russian majority, current population figures include a substantial Muslim minority hailing from Azerbaijan, Dagestan, and several Central Asian states. These construction workers and traders attend the world's northernmost mosque, founded in 1998 and financed by a Tatar native of Noril'sk who since has decamped to Sochi, the resort city on the Black Sea (Paxton, 2007). Meanwhile, the fortunes of Noril'sk Nickel (Nornickel) have improved in recent years, with nearly $7 billion in net profits in 2021. On its website, the company touts the measures it has taken to cut sulfur emissions and otherwise improve the environment (Nornickel, 2022).

The "regional coefficient" of the Northern Increment also applied to southern Sakhalin's oblast capital, Iuzhno-Sakhalinsk, after 1945. Soviet citizens could replace the departing Japanese by pursuing careers and achieve a standard of living higher than almost anywhere else in the country. They in turn sometimes initiated chains of migration by inviting siblings and friends to join them. One such instance, related to us in 2010 by their daughter, Irina Lukka of the Finnish National Library, involved Viktor and Nina. Viktor knew about Sakhalin from his sister Valentina, who had happily settled there with her three children after migrating from the city of Vladimir near Moscow. Discharged from the army, Viktor decided to relocate rather than returning to his job in Moscow. There, he met Nina at a dance. She too had been summoned by a sibling who had exulted, "Here, it's paradise." A specialist in Russian literature and fine arts, Nina found work in her specialty. Irina adds that young professionals also came from Khabarovsk and elsewhere in the Russian Far East as well as Moscow and Leningrad (Siegelbaum and Moch, 2014: 142).

Up to this point, we have used the term "resettlement" (in Russian *pereselenie*) to refer to the migration of rural dwellers to areas where labor was in short supply and industries such as forestry, mining, and fisheries were on the state's agenda for expansion. In Soviet discourse, the term had broader applicability. The NKVD-MGB and other authorities in charge of the deportations officially employed the term "resettlement" in preference to "deportation" (*deportatsiia*; *vysylka*), "eviction" (*vyselenie*), "exile" (*vssylka*), or "expulsion" (*izgnanie*), probably to obscure the difference between coerced and voluntary migration. In reality, the two forms worked in tandem. The lands involuntarily vacated by deportees "needed" new settlers and, given the green light by the Kremlin, resettlement administrators provided the incentives and the wherewithal.

Although not publicly acknowledged, they aimed to "slavicize" newly acquired (or reacquired) territories: Bessarabia and Northern Bukovina, which comprised the Moldavian SSR, formed in 1940 and restored in 1944; and the Baltic region made up of the Estonian, Latvian, and Lithuanian SSRs, Karelia (the ASSR as well as the isthmus lying within Leningrad oblast) and Kaliningrad oblast squeezed between Lithuania and Poland. Wartime losses through death in battle, civilian casualties, the Holocaust, evacuation, flight to the west, and deportation to the east created opportunities for postwar resettlement from other parts of the country. Among the 8.5 million veterans who received their discharges between June 1945 and the end of 1948, quite a few made these borderland territories their new home. For example, Narva, on Estonia's northeastern border with the RSFSR, crops up in several of the interviews conducted with veterans for the Russian website Iremember.ru. To obtain jobs and housing, some relied on friends they had made while serving, others on relatives who had settled there. Interviewees mention as sources of employment the giant Kreenholm textile mill that dated back to the mid-nineteenth century and the brand new (as of 1947) Baltic metalworks factory (Siegelbaum and Moch, 2014: 217–21).

Demobilized soldiers and others seeking a higher standard of living contributed to the significant increase in the numbers and proportion of non-titular groups, particularly Russians, as recorded in successive censuses. If in 1934, Russians comprised a mere 8.2 percent of Estonia's population, then in 1959, they made up 20 percent, their actual numbers rising from 92,500 to 240,200 over this period. The same trend held in the Latvian SSR. The 1935 census had recorded 206,500 Russians representing 10.6 percent of the total population, but in 1959, Russians numbered some 550,000 or 26.6 percent. By 1970, non-Latvian nationalities made up 43 percent of the republic's population, a figure that would increase to 48 percent by 1989. Except for a community indigenous to the Latgale in the country's southeast, most Russians gravitated to the major cities – Riga, the capital, and Daugavpils – where they worked in industry. By 1970, Russians alone outnumbered Latvians in Riga, a gap that would grow to nearly 100,000 by 1989 (Vsesoiuznaia perepis', 1970 and 1989).

The Lithuanian SSR did not replicate this pattern. There, throughout the postwar decades, Russians comprised under 10 percent of the population. More striking, in Vilnius, the capital, Lithuanians went from a tiny minority when the city belonged to Poland before the war to just more than half of the population by 1989. "This can only be understood," writes Tim Snyder, "against the background of the liquidation of Jewish and Polish culture in Vilne/Wilno" thanks to the Holocaust and the resettlement/"repatriation" of Poles "directed locally by Lithuanian communists." The efflux of urban Poles coincided with an influx of Lithuanian peasants and a corresponding proliferation of Lithuanian-language institutions. Snyder also mentions "Lithuania's slow industrialization in the 1950s," which "favored local migration to the capital rather than the massive pan-Soviet influx experienced in Tallinn, Riga, and Minsk" (Snyder, 2003: 92–5).

The breakup of the Soviet Union stranded the Slavic-speaking minorities, which in the cases of Latvia and Estonia were so large and so heavily concentrated in urban districts that they had little incentive to learn the titular language. With independence came laws restricting citizenship to those who passed exams in the history, national anthem, and language of the new nation-state. Slavic speakers thus faced stark choices: learn a language remote from their own to obtain the rights of citizens, live in limbo, or emigrate back to Russia. The third option was complicated partly because the standard of living in Russia was considerably lower, and partly because only the now elderly had left Russia in the first place. Latvia as of 2015 contained some 280,000 people – 13 percent of the country's 2.1 million residents – who were essentially without civil rights, ineligible to vote or hold public office. Still, the majority eventually adapted. Tatiana Makarova, who arrived in Latvia as a six-year-old with her mother in

1952, is among the 71 percent of Russians who by 2015 did what was required to obtain citizenship. Employed in a Riga telephone factory, she spoke fluent Latvian. Although she still considered herself Russian, she claims she "always felt comfortable here" (Williams, 2015).

In Estonia, the constitution curbed the "civil and political rights of" such "noncitizens and stateless persons," who even in the late 1990s, came to 28 percent of that country's population. Overwhelmingly Russian (as in the case of Latvia), 40 percent of Estonia's stateless residents had been born there (Zevelev, 2001: 104–5, 112–15). They absorb Russian-language media from across the border and remain potential pawns in Putin's geopolitical games.

We have traced in Soviet archives the peregrinations of settlers to Karelia after the Winter War of 1939–40 and again following the Great Patriotic War. The first collective-farm settlers arrived in Vyborg from the Russian interior in July 1940. By fall, contingents from Tula, Riazan', and Kyiv oblasts as well as the Chuvash ASSR had arrived. "Pitiable – poor, badly dressed, with many children" was how a junior military officer described those from the Chuvash ASSR whom he was accompanying. Those who found themselves assigned to settlements near the (new) border with Finland expressed alarm at the possibility of attacks. As well they might, for in July–August 1941, Finnish troops retook this territory – but only temporarily.

In 1944, the Soviet army returned, and not long thereafter, the USSR Council of People's Commissars instructed the transport commissariat to send back ("reevacuate") and the commissariat of trade to feed up to 43,000 settlers. Each territorial unit that had absorbed the evacuees from Karelia in 1941 received a quota of people to send back. Despite competing demands to reevacuate settlers to the Latvian and Estonian SSRs, the authorities in the Chuvash ASSR managed to overfulfill their quota of 1,390 people, obtaining volunteers from twenty-six different districts and the republic's capital city of Cheboksary.

Simultaneously, the State Defense Committee assumed responsibility for resettling the Karelian isthmus which, with the Finnish capitulation, had become absorbed within Leningrad oblast. On January 15, 1945, it set a target of signing up "a thousand of the best collective farm families from Vologda, Yaroslavl', and Kirov oblasts." Eight recruiters fanned out across these and other oblasts in search of worthy settlers. Seven million rubles was set aside to subsidize the operation. Already in March, a group of new settlers from four collective farms in the Iaskii (Jääski) district was promising to "energetically (strive to) be ready for spring sowing and develop animal husbandry." Whether Ingrian Finns, the original inhabitants deported to Siberia, were eligible to participate remained a vexed question at least until July 1948. That was when a senior member of Leningrad oblast's executive committee reported that the Party's central committee wanted the districts to be "settled first of all (*prezhde vsego*) by Russian people." Alas, charged with the task of feeding the city of Leningrad, whose surviving population was still recovering from a 900-day siege, the initial Russian settlers disappointed, hence, the resort to a familiar source – demobilized soldiers. Promised loans of 5,000 rubles per family and other incentives, recruits came from as far away as Kazakhstan and the Altai and Omsk krais of Siberia (Stepakov and Balashov, 2001: 35–8, 42; Siegelbaum and Moch, 2014: 49–53).

And so, to Kaliningrad, the former Königsberg, came hundreds of thousands of Soviet settlers, but not immediately. For more than a year after the Potsdam Conference had awarded this sliver of East Prussia to the Soviet Union, it existed as an enclave of stateless Germans, poorly fed and otherwise subjected to ill treatment by Soviet authorities. The first settlers arrived in August 1946, and by the end of the year, more than 12,000 families with 59,000 members had made the move. Like those who settled in the Baltic republics, they came predominantly from the land-poor (*malozemel'nye*) rural areas of the European Russian oblasts, as well as the Chuvash, Mari, and Mordvin autonomous republics, and the Ukrainian and Belarusian SSRs (GARF f. 327, op. 1, d. 90, ll. 22, 191–2; op. 2, d. 442, ll. 21–8, 68; op. 2, d. 609, ll. 5–12).

Regulations permitted settlers to bring livestock, poultry, and bee colonies as part of their personal possessions, and records show that cows accompanied nearly 80 percent of the families. But by March 1947, the official in charge of resettlement for Kaliningrad oblast was reporting that many settlers had slaughtered their livestock, even pregnant cows, because food was in such short supply. Apparently, recruiters had given settlers "an inaccurate representation of the real situation," which was that conditions were "worse than those they left behind." For his part, the oblast's first Party secretary, Ivanov, complained to Stalin in May 1947 that the other parts of the RSFSR had "sent their dregs to Kaliningrad." Nevertheless, settlers kept on coming. By 1951, they numbered some 41,500 families with 188,500 members (Eaton, 2020: 61–2, 66; Maslov, Baranova, and Lopatin, 2022: 37–42, 50). As for the oblast's cities – Kaliningrad and Baltiisk (the former Pillau) – soldiers and sailors, both in service and veterans, plus their families fit the bill. There they persist, an almost exclusively Russian exclave cut off, since 1991, from the rest of the country.

At the opposite end of the country, another territorial acquisition from the Great Patriotic War beckoned settlers. Just as the Karelian isthmus and Kaliningrad became Soviet with the defeat of the enemy in Europe, so South Sakhalin came under Soviet rule with Japan's defeat. And, just as Soviet authorities eventually expelled the German population of the former

Königsberg, so soon after the war's end, they repatriated the resident Japanese to Japan. Eager to restore/develop the oblast's agricultural and fishing industries, resettlement recruiters got to work promoting South Sakhalin.

One can follow the progress – at least on paper – in the archives. The Council of Ministers resolved in March 1947 to recruit 500 collective farm families from Kirov, Voronezh, Gor'kii, and Kursk oblasts to settle on land suitable for agriculture, and 1,800 families from Siberia and the Russian Far East to establish the fishing facilities so important to Sakhalin's economy. Duly recruited, the families with livestock and baggage assembled in Vladivostok and other Far Eastern ports but experienced delays due to inadequate shipping. A memo from July reported disease among the cattle and an "unhealthy attitude" among the settlers and urged the deputy chair of the USSR Council of Ministers, Anastas Mikoian, to "lean on the [Naval] Ministry." Evidence of such leaning is unavailable, but by the end of the year, another memo reported that 1,809 fishing families and 1,065 agricultural kolkhoz families had arrived (GARF f. 327, op. 2, d. 442, ll. 7, 124, 130).

Along the Amur River basin dividing the USSR from China lay another area of settlement, what had become in 1934 the Jewish Autonomous Oblast (JAO) with its capital at Birobidzhan. Intending the JAO as an alternative homeland to Palestine, the Society for Settling Toiling Jews on the Land (Obschestvo zemleustroistva evreiskikh trudiashchikhsia) (OZET) sponsored a campaign that included posters, Yiddish-language novels, a full-length feature film (*Seekers of Happiness*, 1936) and an airdrop of leaflets over Jewish neighborhoods in the Belarusian SSR. Before the war, the Jewish population peaked at a modest 20,000, a reflection not of poor advertising, but of the affinities Soviet Jews had for their places of residence, jobs, and colleagues outside the designated homeland (Pereltsvaig, 2014). After the war, renewed efforts netted additional settlers. Letters between oblast and central authorities in 1947 discussed financial arrangements to support new Jewish settlement, including a contingent of 850 "workers, kolkhozniki, and intelligentsia" from Crimea. From Kherson and Nikolaev oblasts in Ukraine came requests by 1,941 Jewish families who had survived the Holocaust (GARF f. 327, op. 2, d. 441, ll. 1, 224; d. 442, ll. 7, 117). The Jewish population thereby peaked in 1948 at nearly 50,000, constituting a quarter of the oblast's aggregate population (Holley, 2005).

The immediate postwar years saw not only lands vacated by deportees filling up with new settlers, but others marked for infrastructural improvement and economic development claiming their share. Just as the Great Fergana Canal, constructed in 1940, made possible the expansion of cotton growing in Uzbekistan's Fergana Valley, so did the Mingachevir Dam on the Kura River in Azerbaijan make the Kura-Araks lowlands suitable for cultivating that crop on a large scale. But if the Fergana Canal relied on Uzbek *dehqon* (peasant) labor, the shortage of such manpower in the Kura-Araks precipitated extensive vertical coordination between central and republic-level bureaucracies. The process began in December 1947 when the respective Party first secretaries of Azerbaijan and Armenia proposed to "Comrade Stalin" the voluntary resettlement of Armenian-based Azeris to the Kura-Araks region of the Azerbaijan SSR. This transfer of people identified by nationality from one union republic to another distinguished this project from many others during and after the war, such as the RSFSR's expansion of its fishing industry via the recruitment of new settlers from within the republic (Siegelbaum and Moch, 2014: 53; Goff, 2022: 97–108).

Within a month of the proposal, the Council of Ministers had produced a decree authorizing voluntary resettlement of 100,000 Azeris on a three-year schedule. As detailed by Krista Goff, respective union- and regional-level bureaucracies made the necessary financial arrangements, advertised extensively, arranged transportation, and provided material incentives. Prospective settlers in turn sent scouts to choose specific destinations. All this is reminiscent of Soviet resettlement regimes. So too was the failure of the expected number of recruits to show up at collection points (thus sabotaging the fulfillment of targets set by the Resettlement Administration) and the eventual return of many who did participate (Goff, 2022: 101, 107–9).

Nationality complicates this case in two ways. First, part of the logic behind the plan was that Azeris' departure would make more room for Armenian repatriates. Second, the way many resettlers came to understand their displacement and its associated disappointments was through the lens of nationality, namely that Armenians were expelling them. The evidence suggests otherwise. This undertaking relocated mountain dwellers to a different habitat – cotton fields – where they found summers unbearably hot. But the economic basis for resettlement failed to register in the Azeri national memory, which is why it figures in the tensions and periodic outright warfare between the two neighboring former Soviet republics.

Azerbaijan is a good example of a Union republic within the USSR where those willing to work on behalf of the titular nation employed it as an organizing principle to enhance their own power and bargaining position with central authorities in Moscow. This strategy, as Goff and others have argued, had serious implications in the 1930s for the non-titular nationalities, including their loss of access to cultural and material resources and, in the case of some, even more traumatic consequences. While the Tats, a Persian-speaking people, were subjected to forced assimilation into the Azerbaijani nationality, Kurds experienced both compulsory assimilation and, in 1937, deportation to Kazakhstan. A similar dynamic, including stereotyping of Kurds as among the "backward" national minorities (*natsmen*), led to their expulsion from Armenia in the same year (Goff, 2020, 10–12).

As we have noted already, moving people to where resources needed development served as a central objective of Soviet authorities. Whereas the Stalin era featured forced migration, alternative approaches became more prominent thereafter when officials in remote parts of the country seeking to develop underutilized lands competed to entice collective farmers. They did so in the 1950s and early 1960s by commissioning posters and brochures typically titled "Come Settle with Us in _____." A collection of them at the Russian National Library in St. Petersburg significantly enhanced our appreciation of this effort. Each brochure enthused about its advertised region, listed the benefits to settlers, and glowed with accounts by those who already had settled. Sakhalin's claimed the island as "The Jewel of the Far East." Fedor Sodovnik who came from Ukraine's Poltava oblast admitted that "It is very far from Poltava, but . . . we live well and in a cultured fashion . . . Our collective farm is six kilometers from the district center next to a railroad." Sodovnik enumerated the club, seven-year school, medical station, and three stores in the village. The farm itself, he proudly exclaimed, "has electricity and radio" (Kheifets, 1955: 7).

Another brochure promoting western Kazakhstan countered with the claim that "the steppe is always beautiful – in spring when it is covered by thick grasses, in summer when waves of grain resemble the sea, and in winter under a blanket of sparkling white snow." As it happens, this brochure also contained appeals from former Poltava oblast residents who assured their compatriots that they would "find everything to your liking. You will be at home, and at work you will earn a lot" (*Pereseliates' v zapadnyi Kazakhstan*, 1960: 2). Resettlement recruiters offered temptations all over, from Petrozavodsk in Soviet Karelia to Kemerovo and Tomsk in central Siberia, Krasnoiarsk farther to the east, and Khabarovsk krai deep in the Russian Far East.

The Virgin Lands (*tselina*) program, which recruited more than 300,000 volunteers to cultivate grain in the west Siberian and northern Kazakh steppe, dwarfed all these programs. The Communist Party's youth organization, the Komsomol, took the leading role as recruiters. Young Russians and Ukrainians either eager for adventure or desperate to escape poverty and boredom responded to the appeal to resettle farther to the east. What they encountered became the stuff of legend. One *tselinnik* recalled years later living in a dugout with "bad" food and water, the wind blowing constantly, his skin peeling from sunburn, and snakes. And yet "we were happy, such songs we sang!" Another described the steppe as "so big that one's spirit seized up from the unbelievable emptiness." "How strange," she added, "to feel oneself on this absolute flatness as the smallest grain of sand." With time, however, "this feeling of being lost and orphaned passed and was replaced by feelings of certainty and freedom." Emptiness, the elements, and freedom comprised key components of Virgin Land mythology that celebrated the willingness of volunteers to "go where nobody has gone before, to live where nobody has lived before, to work where nobody has worked before," like cosmonautics or "any endeavor involving a quest, a consciousness of the unexplored, a necessity to begin" (Konov, 1974; Makarov, 1974).

The scheme originally called for the plowing of millions of acres of virgin soil – 47 million in 1954 alone – but, encouraged by initial results, Khrushchev signed off on an additional 35 million for 1955. The quintessential Soviet program in which people of different nationalities relocated for every kind of reason and came together in a common Herculean task, its sheer magnitude almost invited problems. Drought, persistent housing shortages, and other logistical shortcomings endemic to frontier societies required mobilizations of 100,000 people every year during the mid-1950s just to compensate for departures. Clashes – scuffles at social gatherings, knife fights, and even communal riots between new settlers and the residue of earlier forced migrations as well as indigenous Kazakhs also occurred. Yet, among those who stuck it out, the *tselina* offered a second chance in life, the opportunity to intermingle and even to intermarry with those who came before them or were native to the region, inspiring a veteran *tselinnik* to look back nostalgically from 1994 and describe it as "a new planet" where "communism . . . had already started" (Pohl, 2007: 245–55).

Nothing like this ever happened again. Subsequent state projects for agricultural development focused on raising productivity through mechanization, a key strategy in overcoming rural out-migration. Common to much of the European continent, the rural exodus in the Soviet Union was particularly evident in the Central Economic Region around Moscow. From 1959 to 1973 its rural areas lost 4.1 million able-bodied people, of whom nearly two-thirds were between twenty and twenty-nine years old. Mechanization did not fully compensate and thus the problem of adequate labor inputs continued. A resolution of the Party's Central Committee from 1974 envisioned consolidation of "villages without a future" (*neperspektivnye derevny*), specifically in the Central Economic Region (Kommunisticheskaia partiia, 1983–90: 405; Siegelbaum, 2016: 43–58).

A rather inventive initiative supplementing this effort consisted of recruiting rurals from Uzbekistan to improve land and construct housing in connection with the establishment of three fully functioning state farms: "Tashkent" and

"Friendship" in Novgorod oblast, and "Uzbekistan" in Ivanovo oblast. Conceived as a pilot program, it appeared to kill two birds with one stone: reducing under-employment among Uzbek collective farmers on one hand and helping to solve the agricultural labor supply problem in European Russia on the other. So promising did the scheme appear, that it spawned others – in Smolensk oblast, the Chuvash ASSR, the new oil-and-gas complex around Tiumen' in western Siberia, and the Maritime oblast in the Far East. But for all the talk of a "second Virgin Lands," the numbers of Uzbeks willing to subject themselves to radically different cultures and climates was small (Fierman, 1991: 255–6, 277–82).

At the same time, however, highly educated and urban-based people from Central Asia and the Caucasus seized opportunities to leave their native repub-lics, if only temporarily, for the largest and most cosmopolitan of Soviet cities, Moscow and Leningrad. In doing so, they partook of the ideology of the "friendship of the peoples" (*druzhba narodov*), one of the most frequently invoked slogans in Party propaganda. The propaganda infused festivals, cele-brating the richness of each titular nationality's culture and its contributions to Soviet life, thereby providing a sense of belonging. Interviewed decades later by Jeff Sahadeo and his team of researchers, many such migrants from the southern and eastern parts of the country fondly recalled their youthful participation in Soviet public life – that is, Party-sponsored activities and educational institu-tions. These experiences at home primed them for seeking advancement within the wider context of the "two capital cities" (Sahadeo, 2019).

Soviet policies and practices facilitated their migration. Those who sought further education benefited from the quotas that reserved places for them at the most prestigious institutes and universities. With acceptance came dormitory accommodation and the highly sought-after residence permit (*propiska*). Moreover, they could travel between their homelands and the cities without great inconvenience or expense. In addition to the railroad, travel by airplane grew prodigiously. Domestic airplane traffic rose from 16 million passengers in 1960 to 70 million in 1970 and 96 million five years later. By 1975, eight scheduled flights a day connected Erevan, the Armenian capital, to Moscow. The trip cost 34 rubles while the average monthly wage throughout the USSR was 135 rubles. Flights from Tbilisi numbered nine per day for 31 rubles. One had to pay 48 rubles to fly from more distant Tashkent, but one could take the train for as little as 26 rubles. Tajik Saodat-Opa, whom we last met at her wedding, recalled, "You could travel anywhere you wanted, get on a train and ride to Moscow if you wanted without even taking your passport with you!" (Reeves, 2007: 281; Siegelbaum and Moch, 2016: 984–5).

Although assisted by the Soviet state, migrants to Moscow and Leningrad also relied on their own repertoires of migration, including the tried-and-true institution of *zemliaki* (home area associations) and friendships that cut across national distinctions. Sevda Asgarova, recruited from Azerbaijan in the 1950s to study at a higher Party school in Moscow, recalled that she "had friends from various ethnicities: Russians, Kabardins, people of mixed blood. And I associated with every ethnic group." The 1977 film comedy *Mimino* told the tale of one such easy friendship in Moscow between an aspiring Armenian pilot and a Georgian truck driver. Such relationships occurred in an atmosphere sullied by resentment. Admissions quotas and public queuing for consumer goods in short supply exposed Central Asians and people from the Caucasus to bitterness tinged with racism from ordinary Muscovites as well as university professors (Daneliya, 1977; Sahadeo, 2019: 92–115, 206–9).

As material life began to deteriorate in the 1980s, the racism grew more pronounced. This coincided with the growing presence of ethnically distinct traders from the south and east. Of the sixteen interviewees Sahadeo identified as traders, none arrived before 1980. Spotted at markets, kiosks, and train stations, they offered fresh produce, flowers, videos, and a range of other goods to an increasingly bewildered public. The police harassed them by repeatedly checking their papers, demanding bribes, and otherwise making their lives difficult. Nonetheless, commercial links survived. The aforementioned Tashkent sovkhoz in Novgorod oblast, which sought to rely on Uzbek cultivators, did not outlive the fall of the Soviet Union, but the land it occupied continued to produce potatoes and vegetables that traders, who came from Uzbekistan and Tajikistan, helped market (Kolotnecha, 2007). By that time, much larger groups of Central Asians were working at unskilled jobs in Russia's major cities, as discussed in Section 3.

3 Entering and Leaving

In the years immediately following the "ten days that shook the world," Soviet Russia projected itself as a haven for workers and intellectuals persecuted in their own countries for their communist political sympathies. John Reed, the most famous, not only reported on but also avidly participated in the political life of the country and the Communist International (Comintern). He succumbed to typhus, however, in 1920. Thousands of others arriving in the land of soviets during the civil war offered their assistance, though not many stayed on for more than a few years. The paramount necessity of economic recovery led the Soviet state in the early 1920s to recruit political sympathizers who possessed technical skills ("know-how"). Among those from North America, "re-emigrants" – that is, former subjects of the Russian empire, responded and were accepted most readily (Sawyer, 2013). Three projects, two industrial and the third agricultural, illustrate the possibilities: the takeover of the AMO automobile factory in Moscow by 123 workers from Ford's Highland Park factory in Detroit; the Kuzbas Industrial Colony (AIK) in Siberia that attracted members of the anarchist labor union, the International Workers of the World (IWW); and agricultural communes situated in southern Russia and Ukraine.

The Ford workers, "accustomed to conditions of mass automated processes that were worked out exactly to the finest detail," could not reproduce them in Moscow. The factory's director, Arthur Adams, stayed in the position for three years, claiming some improvements, but the handful of F-15 trucks the factory turned out did not begin their lives until after his departure (Siegelbaum, 2008: 13–15). The more extensive Kuzbas project, attracting about 750 workers and specialists from a variety of national backgrounds and with a significant representation of women, sought to reconstruct a flooded coal mine and complete the building of a chemical factory. Ben Sawyer argues that those recruited to the colony came not expecting to live in a promised land but to do meaningful work. They did, although bureaucracies working at cross-purposes, logistical problems, and homesickness ate into the initial enthusiasm. Stories by returnees with headlines such as "Wobblies Say Soviet Failure" and "Lies and 'Free Love' Cure U.S. Reds in Russia" titillated newspaper readers in the United States and left a lasting and largely erroneous impression about the project that survived until 1926 (Morray, 1983; Sawyer, 2013: 119, 208–12).

Agricultural communes worked by immigrants from Germany, Italy, Czechoslovakia, and especially the United States and Canada took root about the same time. Bernstein and Cherny estimate their number as between twenty-five and thirty. Intended as model farms, only a few came close to fulfilling the hopes of their founders. Among them, the "Seattle" commune, set up in the Don oblast in 1922, stood out for both its financial soundness and durability. Notwithstanding the local population's initial hostility, continual friction between the Finnish American majority and the less well-endowed Russian Americans, and the departure in 1931 of most of the Finns for Soviet Karelia, "Seattle" managed to carry on until the end of its eighteen-year lease in 1939, long after others – for example, the "California" commune – had dispersed (Ylikangas, 2011: 79; Bernstein and Cherny, 2014: 28, 33–7).

In moving to Karelia, the former members of the Seattle commune joined some 6,500 of their ethnic kin who left Depression-wracked North America between 1931 and 1934 (Saramo, 2022). A considerably larger number of Finns – estimated at 12,000 – also caught "Karelian fever" and illegally crossed into the Soviet Union as "border hoppers" (*loikkarit* in Finnish) in order to escape worsening economic conditions at home. Terry Martin understands these arrivals as the fruit of what he terms "the Piedmont Principle" – "the policy of clustering national groups near borders to project political influence into neighboring states" (Martin, 2001: 8–9). Beginning in 1935, Ingrian Finns, deported from Leningrad oblast, further swelled the Finnish population of Karelia. This mixing of free and coerced migration streams made for complicated relations, as already observed in northern Kazakhstan and, indeed, elsewhere in the USSR (Lam, 2010, 211–12).

Other contingents of Americans came as technical specialists to assist the Soviet Union in developing its economy during the First Five-Year Plan. Most stayed for a limited period, applying their skills to specific industrial projects such as the construction of Magnitogorsk's blast furnaces, Dneprostroi, and the auto plant outside Nizhni-Novgorod before returning home. The group of sixteen Americans who arrived in Leningrad in November 1931 were different in at least two respects: they were agrarian specialists, and they were African Americans. Recruited with the assistance of George Washington Carver, they signed on with Amtorg, the Soviet commercial agency, from a variety of motives – to escape poverty and racial segregation, to utilize the skills they had learned at Tuskegee, to see the world.

Experts in growing cotton, the group traveled to Uzbekistan where, some 60 kilometers from Tashkent, they established a colony (or "collective") for experimenting with cross-bred seeds. After the expiration of their contract in 1934, everyone signed up for another three years. But by 1937, confronted with the choice of returning to the United States or becoming Soviet citizens, most chose the first option. Oliver Golden and his wife, Bertha, decided to stay. Born in Mississippi, Oliver attended (but did not graduate from) Tuskegee, served in France during World War I, briefly worked as a Pullman waiter based in Chicago, and then, in 1921, decided to further his education at the Communist University of the Toilers of the East (Kommunisticheskii universitet trudiashchikhsia Vostoka) (KUTV) in Moscow. He returned home in 1927, but within a few years was organizing black agricultural specialists to improve Soviet cotton production. Bertha, Oliver's wife, had arrived in the United States in 1920 as a teenager from Warsaw. According to her granddaughter Yelena, her decision to marry a *schvartze* alienated her from her family. Likewise, the birth of a daughter – Yelena's mother – in Tashkent in 1934 was decisive in the couple's decision to become Soviet citizens, for "they did not want to raise a racially mixed child in America" (Khanga, 1992: 42–9, 52–4, 72–4, 83–6).

Who else found haven in the Soviet Union during these years? Communists fleeing political persecution. They came from many European countries as well as Asia – from Germany, Italy, Spain, and France, from Poland, Hungary, and Bulgaria, from China and French Indochina – making the USSR a virtual Communist Mecca. Some of the world's leading Communists such as China's Liu Shaoqi and Vietnam's Ho Chi Minh studied in Moscow in the 1920s. During the 1930s, leading Communists escaped arrest or worse at the hands of fascist regimes in their own countries by going to work for the Comintern in the Soviet capital. Among them was Bulgarian Georgi Dimitrov who, after his acquittal in the Leipzig (Reichstag fire) trial, obtained Soviet citizenship. He spent the next twelve years in the Soviet Union, from 1935 until its dissolution in 1943, as general secretary of the Comintern. Hungarian Marxist philosopher György Lukàcs arrived in Moscow in 1930 and also worked for the Comintern when not engaged in familiarizing himself at the Marx-Engels Institute with the unpublished works of the young Marx. After evacuation to Tashkent, he would return to Hungary in 1944 (Stankova, 2010; Lukacs, 2013). Both Palmiro Togliatti, secretary of the Italian Communist Party, and Maurice Thorez, his counterpart in France, spent the war years in Moscow. Spanish Communist leaders José Diaz and Dolores Ibárruri (la Pasionaria) also came to the USSR in 1939 and went to work for the Comintern. Both were evacuated to Tbilisi after the Nazi invasion. Diaz died there, evidently from suicide; Ibárruri repatriated to Spain in 1977.

German and Austrian Communists comprised a sufficiently large group in Moscow to sustain the Karl Liebknecht School, which opened in 1924 to educate their children. After the Nazis came to power, enrollment swelled, reaching 750 in the 1934–5 school year. In summer, children of German expatriates could attend the Ernst Thälmann camp, named after the German Communist Party leader imprisoned by the Nazis. Its alumni included Wolfgang Leonhard, future Yale University historian of international communism, and Markus Wolf, future head of the foreign intelligence section of the German Democratic Republic's (GDR) Ministry of State Security, better known as the Stasi. Both repatriated to (East) Germany after the war. The summer of 1934 brought another group of German-speaking kids to Moscow, orphans of members of the Schutzbund killed during the brief Austrian civil war. "Said a Soviet spokesman, 'These children will be sent first to vacation camps and then to schools as proteges of the Soviet Union'" (*Time*, 1934).

Did any of them rub shoulders with *los niños de Rusia*, the children of Communists and other supporters of the republic besieged by Franco's forces during the Spanish Civil War? Some 2,895 children, shipped mostly from the Basque region and Asturias in 1937–8 and accompanied by about 150 adult educators and medical personnel, received a warm welcome upon arriving in Soviet ports. Indeed, they were a centerpiece of what Glennys Young has called "Soviet espanophilia." Distributed among boarding schools (*casas de niños*) located for the most part near major Soviet Russian and Ukrainian cities, the children received an education in Spanish with an eye to their return to Spain, assuming Franco's defeat (see Figure 4). The triumph of the Falange, however,

Figure 4 Spanish refugee children in Soviet young pioneer camp, late 1930s

meant the children stayed on after 1939. They and hundreds of evacuated Spanish aviators and sailors would share the full range of wartime experiences with Soviet citizens: service in the Red Army and the People's Militia, hunger, evacuation, and death (Young, 2014: 404; Qualls, 2020).

After the war, those who survived pursued a wide range of careers as factory workers, artists, engineers, and scientists. Perhaps the best-known among them was Agustín Gómez (1922–75), a soccer standout who played for Moscow Torpedo, captaining the team in the early 1950s. Repatriation to Spain began even during the war with a few POWs. Boatloads of returnees began departing in 1957, and, within a year, approximately half of the *niños* were back in their native country. Treated with suspicion by Spanish authorities and restricted in many ways, several hundred opted to return to the USSR. In the 1960s, about 200 *hispano-soviéticos* took up positions as Soviet specialists in Cuba. One source claims that 239 of the *niños* were still living in the former Soviet republics as of 2004 (Young, 2014). Their example points to a central irony of "home" turning out to feel like anything but home and diasporic life being preferable.

In the summer of 1944, as the Red Army pushed west through Ukraine into Poland, the Soviet government reached an agreement with the newly created Polish government in Lublin to arrange an exchange of populations between the two states. Ethnic Poles residing in the USSR would move west and Ukrainians and Belarusians would travel in the opposite direction. Here, we will address the eastward migration of more than a half million civilians from 1944 through 1947. Based on self-identification, Ukrainians and Belarusians living in eastern Polish provinces would join their ethnic kin in respective Soviet republics. However, rooted in their homes and villages, quite a few designated for the transfer resented the displacement and loss of community ties. Intended as a voluntary program, it ended up requiring "psychological pressure, physical intimidation and economic sanctions" to persuade the targeted populations.

New arrivals primarily consisted of peasant households with a distinct minority of artisans and industrial and white-collar workers. Children and old people made up 40 percent and women outnumbered men. As to the reception, one scholar notes, "Different parts of what was becoming a single Belarusian nation did not recognize each other when they first came in contact, and, after moving to Belarus, the resettlers were often called 'Poles.'" In Ukraine, there were reports of local kids beating up resettlers' children, newcomers facing locals' hostility ("Go back to Poland"), and terrible poverty. Yet, despite this rough treatment, the general paucity of resources, and resettlers' occasional efforts to reverse direction, the transfer met official expectations (Stadnik, 2009: 176–7; Halavach, 2021: 21–2).

Elsewhere in the Soviet Union, another motherland was calling its sons and daughters home. In November 1945, Stalin issued an invitation to Armenians living abroad to immigrate, accompanied by extensive propaganda portraying the Armenian SSR as a "homeland." Civil war in Greece, and poor economic conditions in Lebanon, Syria, elsewhere in Southeastern Europe, and the Near East made the invitation particularly attractive. Parts of the diaspora returned, inspired by the Soviet victory and promises of assistance. They included several thousand from France. In December 1946, when the newcomers were arriving in droves, *Pravda* reported that "Hundreds of people fell to their knees, took the smooth, sunburned earth into their hands and kissed it." By 1949, between 90,000 and 110,000 Armenians – about 10 percent of all Armenians living outside the Soviet Union – had migrated, most via ship convoys that docked at Batumi in neighboring Georgia. Roughly half settled on collective farms, while Erevan, Leninakan (since 1991 Gyumri), and smaller cities absorbed the other half (Laycock, 2009; Lehmann, 2012: 171–2; GARF f. 327, op. 1, d. 2).

Maike Lehmann's analysis of interviews, memoirs, and archival material makes evident the difficulties of their integration. Soviet authorities sought to confiscate repatriates' Bibles and other "problematic books" they brought with them. At work, locals blamed repatriates for any mishap. Because of repatriates' unfamiliarity with the Eastern Armenian language used throughout the republic, locals considered them illiterate. Little wonder that soon after arriving dozens of repatriates fled across the border to Turkey. And, of the 67,000 Armenians deported to Siberia and Central Asia in 1949–50 because of supposed Dashnak affiliations, three-quarters were repatriates, which means one out of two repatriates experienced a double displacement. Nevertheless, as Lehmann acutely observes, an anecdote commonly told among repatriates that partook of a genre of Soviet humor itself indicates their "partial integration and adaptation to Soviet Armenian society." After kissing the earth of her new "homeland," a repatriated woman discovers that someone has walked off with her bag (Lehmann, 2012: 195, 198, 199, 205, 207, 210).

About a decade later, following in the footsteps of two smaller groups of repatriates (1935, 1947), roughly 100,000 Russians "returned" from China whence their parents and grandparents had settled. Many had worked for the Chinese Eastern Railroad and lived in Harbin, Manchuria, a Russian colony. Very few were sympathetic to Communism. Despite repression of previous returnees in the mid-1930s when Japan took over the railroad, the Soviet victory in World War II, the establishment of the People's Republic of China in 1949, and Stalin's death in 1953 encouraged many to make the move. Why? The appeal of the Motherland trumped staying where they were or moving to yet another alien society. Memoirists and those interviewed by Laurie Manchester acknowledge that they imagined returning to their homeland, a sentiment particularly strong among the younger generation born in China.

Apparently, the Soviet state accepted all comers. Promised free transport and "several thousand rubles of start-up money" per family, the "Chinese Russians" found themselves in reduced and rural circumstances upon arrival, having been directed to state farms in the Virgin Lands. They immediately stood out for the clothes they wore, their comportment, and propensity to engage in Old World practices like men kissing women's hands in public. Their sense of otherness, of being "strangers among their own," as one repatriate entitled his memoir, lasted long after they had moved on to live urban lives and enter professions. The feeling even survived the Soviet Union. As late as 1999, Vladimir Borodin, who had migrated to the Soviet Union from Tientsin in 1947 at age eleven, remarked that "It is Russia now, but most people are not really Russians, they are still Soviets way deep in their hearts and minds. Frankly, I just can't get over the idea, though I know it is ridiculous, that real Russians were in China, the emigrants of the White Army" (Manchester, 2007: 359, 368).

By then, the distinctiveness of the Chinese Russians had faded because, with the dissolution of the Soviet Union, some 3 million ethnic Russians had arrived from the other former Soviet republics (Ivakhnyuk, 2009: 16). Administrators, industrial managers, and professionals who had made their lives outside the RSFSR, they represented "children of empire." In this sense, they conformed to what migration historian Leo Lucassen has termed "the reversal of fate principle" that left Hungarians outside Hungary after the collapse of the Dual Monarchy and the Pieds-Noirs in the former north African colonies of France (Leo Lucassen, private correspondence, 2013). But the "aftermath of empire" framing of Russians' "return" migration is only one prism through which to view this massive process. Taking a broader chronological perspective, the reversal of Russian migration actually began in the 1960s, first in the Caucasus, and then by the 1980s, in Central Asia as well. It can be correlated with the shift in investment strategy from those areas to the north and the Russian Far East, the increasing "nativization" of political power along with greater autonomy from Moscow, and even a rise in interethnic tensions prompting complaints to central authorities from, for example, Russians living in Uzbekistan (Austin, 2023: chap. 1).

However, successive census data suggest that the pattern of Russians returning to the RSFSR did not hold for all the non-Russian republics. In Soviet Ukraine, the number of people who declared themselves Russian increased from 7 million in 1959 to 10.4 million in 1979 and 11.3 million in 1989. But during the 1990s, this number decreased by some 3 million, partly because people redefined themselves as Ukrainian, partly because Russians emigrated, and partly as a result of natural attrition. That decade saw an estimated 9 million people, mainly but not only Russians, leaving one former Soviet republic for another. No single factor can account for so much crossing of what had become international borders. Fears of material impoverishment and real economic difficulties; laws and informal practices favoring titular nationals for entry into educational institutions, jobs, and promotions; reduction of prospects for one's children; microaggressions in daily life; concern for safety, and the departure of friends and relatives all pushed people out. "Pull" factors included relative political stability, economic opportunity, cultural familiarity, and accommodating immigration policies (Brubaker, 1995; Itogi perepisi 2001 goda na Ukraine, 2003; Radnitz, 2006: 653).

In the case of the newly constituted Russian Federation, two laws from February 1993 codified ad hoc policies toward Russian nationals and those from other national groups within the former Soviet Union. One defined Russians as "forced migrants" who could exchange their Soviet passports for newly minted ones from the Russian Federation; the other "On Refugees" covered non-Russian nationals either from within former Soviet territory or from the "far abroad." Estimates of the number of people to whom these laws applied range from the official figure of 1.2 million as of January 1998 up to 10 million (Siegelbaum and Moch, 2014: 271). From where did Russians leave? First, we must return to the question of declared nationality. Having Russian nationality in the "near abroad" (the Russian term for the other fourteen former Soviet republics) was an advantage if (a) one descended from a punished people, like the deported Volga Germans or borderland Poles; (b) one wanted easier entry into the Russian Federation. But how many offspring of Germans or Poles declared themselves to be Russian is impossible for us to know.

First and foremost, Russian nationals came from Kazakhstan, which, after Ukraine, contained the largest number outside the RSFSR/Russian Federation. In 1989, more than 6 million Russian nationals lived in the Kazakh SSR, two-thirds of whom had been born there. By 1999, their numbers had dropped to 4.4 million, with the largest annual exodus occurring in 1994, when nearly 350,000 departed. Next came Kyrgyzstan. It lost 197,000 Russians between 1991 and 1995. Although far fewer in number, the Russians who left Moldavia seem to have struck the best deal in negotiating the conditions of their arrival thanks to lobbying by their Center of Russian Culture. They received, for example, official approval for compact settlements in European Russia, long-term interest-free loans, and the treasured *propiska* for urban residence (Peyrouse, 2007; Austin, 2023).

Around the turn of the millennium, as the number of Russians in the "near abroad" diminished, the Russian government began searching for additional immigrants to compensate for population loss. The fruit of its deliberations came in 2006 with the "State program on providing support for voluntary resettlement of compatriots to the Russian Federation." Broadly defined, the program applied to ethnic Russians, Russian speakers, and people "spiritually" and "culturally" linked to the Russian Federation. Among its primary objectives is the promotion of socioeconomic development in regions designated for priority settlement. The most strenuous efforts applied to the Russian Far East, where population decline was particularly acute. That is where Old Believer communities that had departed in the 1920s for the Americas began to settle in 2009. Like the Russians who had returned from China, they embodied a pre-Soviet ideal of Russianness. Their vigorous reproductive patterns and relative prosperity made them ideal to those who, in Lauren Woodard's words, "envisioned the restoration of an imagined past as a solution to an uncertain future" (Woodard, 2020: 99).

The program is still very active. It is reminiscent of "right of return" laws in such countries as Germany and Israel. The number of designated regions, originally twelve, grew to seventy-six by 2020. Under the program's auspices, a total of 530,000 people had received citizenship by the end of 2015, including a substantial contingent of Ukrainians fleeing the conflict in the eastern part of that country. A more recent estimate places the total number of compatriot "returnees" at more than 800,000 (Donets and Chudinovskikh, 2020; Hamed-Troyansky, 2021).

The demand for labor, though, proved far greater, much of it for the kind that both Russians and their compatriots from abroad had come to disdain. The relative stagnation of the other economies in the Commonwealth of Independent States (CIS) and Russia's open-borders policy precipitated a deluge of temporary labor migrants – temporary because bureaucratic strictures blocked paths to legal employment as well as Russian citizenship. Data from the turn of the millennium reveal an enormous disparity between the numbers of officially registered ("regular") migrants and those circumventing regulations ("irregular"). The latter, it is estimated, outnumbered the former by some fourteen times. By country of origin, Ukraine sent the largest group of regulars, some 39 percent, followed distantly by Moldavia, Tajikistan, and Armenia. Among irregulars, Ukraine's proportion stood at 27 percent (Ivakhnyuk, 2009: 31–3, table 5).

Tellingly, the largest gap between numbers of regular and irregular migrants was for groups like the Kyrgyz: 20,000 regulars compared to 350,000–400,000 irregulars, a ratio of at least 1:17. "Like the Kyrgyz" means people from Central Asia and the Caucasus, including those from within the Russian Federation such as Chechens. The racialization of these former Soviet peoples into "people of color" went part and parcel with the ethnicization of low-status and low-wage labor, creating a syndrome familiar to students of postcolonial societies. These were the years when Moscow emerged as a global city with its freewheeling community of expats – "expat" being an upscale version of temporary migrant – and characteristically enormous inequalities of wealth. The successive censuses of 1989 and 2002 reported that the number of Georgians in Moscow more than doubled, that of Armenians grew nearly three times, that of Azeris quadrupled, and that of Central Asians increased ten times over! Working primarily in services, petty trade, and construction, these groups found themselves competing more and more often with migrants from the "far abroad" – that is, from such countries as Turkey, Afghanistan, Iran, Vietnam, and elsewhere in Asia (Roman, 2002; Ivakhnyuk, 2009: 32–3, 39–40; Scott, 2016: 251–2).

Actually, Vietnamese had been coming to Moscow since the 1970s, first as students and vocational trainees, then as workers on one-year labor contracts. The Likhachev Automobile Factory, for example, employed several thousand. By 1987, according to one estimate, almost 100,000 mostly male Vietnamese resided in the USSR working in car plants, textile factories, and other industrial facilities in Moscow, Nizhni Novgorod (Gor'kii), Ekaterinburg (Sverdlovsk), Tomsk, and Vladivostok. Like Turkish and other *Gastarbeiter* in Germany, many had extended their stays by marrying Soviet women, obtaining residence permits by other means, or evading regulations (Ginsburgs, 1989). During the 1990s and especially in the new millennium, restaurants catering to the expat community as well as increasingly venturesome Russians raised the Vietnamese profile, especially in Moscow and St. Petersburg. A bilateral agreement reached in 2008 but taking effect from 2013 once again regularized employment conditions for Vietnamese, providing for the entry of 15,000–20,000 workers per annum (Duc, Hieu, and Hung, 2022: 193–4).

This arrangement followed up on attempts by the Federal Migration Service (FMS) that presides over the execution of migration policy to simplify procedures and otherwise expand opportunities for legal entry into Russia by CIS citizens. From 2006 onwards, migrants from those countries could search for jobs immediately upon arriving in a Russian city, register their residence irrespective of where or whether they worked, change jobs without seeking permission of legal authorities, and in other respects integrate themselves into the general labor market. "Liberalization" and "humanization" serve as the watchwords for the revised policy. Official data suggest it immediately resulted in a sharp increase in work permits issued, with more than half a million going to Uzbeks alone in 2008 (Ivakhnyuk, 2009: 53–4, 60).

Economic and political perturbations notwithstanding, this migration regime continued to prove its effectiveness for another decade or so in the sense of maintaining an adequate, low-wage labor force that earned enough to send remittances home. The COVID-19 pandemic disrupted this arrangement. The imposition of lockdowns in the cities, the closing of Russia's borders, and a corresponding trimming of staff and wages in the private sector led to a sharp decline in the number of temporary migrants employed. Perhaps as many as 5 million returned home. Construction and agriculture suffered the most, followed by hospitality (AFP, 2021; Russia Hit by Fall in Migrant Workers from Central Asia, 2021).

These departures from the Russian Federation remind us of the extensive history of emigration since the October Revolution of 1917. Typically, Soviet-era emigrants are grouped in four "waves." The first, so-called White Russian emigration, occurred during the years of revolution and civil war, when up to 2 million fled the country. Not all were Whites in the sense of having supported the White armies that had sought to overthrow the Bolshevik-led Red Army. But the core consisted of prerevolutionary elites who not only stood to lose property and personal security but also feared for their lives. Political enemies of the

Bolsheviks such as Mensheviks and Socialist Revolutionaries numbered among the emigres too. This wave of emigration washed over Istanbul, Paris, Prague, Harbin, and other cities where exiled Russian communities established churches, schools, newspapers, and other institutions and practices that recreated much of what they had left behind.

Top-flight generals Anton Denikin and Pyotr Wrangel lived in exile, unreconciled to their defeats. In 1924, Wrangel formed the Russian All-Military Union to try to maintain the fighting spirit among military exiles in preparation for another go at the Bolsheviks. That same year, Boris Savinkov, the socialist revolutionary who had instigated rebellions against Bolshevik rule in the summer of 1918, was lured back from exile, put on trial, convicted, and sentenced to ten years' imprisonment. Most other political exiles renounced such activism. The Russian Provisional Government's last prime minister, Alexander Kerensky, for example, immersed himself in the Hoover Institution Archives at Stanford University and authored several studies of the revolution. He lived in France, the United States, and Australia. By contrast, Pavel Miliukov, leader of the Constitutional Democratic (Kadet) Party in successive Dumas, continued to agitate from Paris for the Bolsheviks' overthrow, although he did urge support for the Soviet Union during the Second World War.

The victory of the Bolsheviks proved a boon to the arts abroad, thanks to Russia's extrusion of many painters, writers, musicians, choreographers, and dancers. Some such as Mark Chagall, Wassily Kandinsky, Igor Stravinsky, Serge Rachmaninoff, Sergei Diaghilev, and Vaslav Nijinsky already had well-established international reputations that they burnished after leaving Russia. Sergei Prokofiev, Maxim Gorky, and others left Soviet Russia shortly after the revolution but returned, Gorky in 1931 and Prokofiev five years later, to great acclaim. Still others – writers Vladimir Nabokov and Ivan Bunin, for example – honed their skills abroad, where they essentially made their reputations. Finally, the first wave included "philosophers' ships," German steamers that carried more than 200 leading intellectuals (philosophers Nikolai Berdyaev, Sergei Bulgakov, and Ivan Ilyin, among others, as well as sociologist Pitrim Sorokin) who had run afoul of Lenin (Makarov and Khristoforov, 2003). Unlike those previously mentioned, the "philosophers" were banished rather than leaving of their own accord. This would set a precedent of sorts, followed by the likes of Lev Trotsky, whom Stalin booted out in 1929, and Alexander Solzhenitsyn, whose Soviet citizenship was revoked in 1974.

The narrative of four waves of emigration from the Soviet Union obscures the departures of significant numbers of non-Russians during the intervening decades between the first and second waves. The data are imprecise, but it appears that, between 1923 and 1930, roughly 20,000 Mennonites decamped to Canada and a few thousand others settled in South America (Polian, 2006). Kazakh nomad pastoralists escaping forced "sedentarization" and famine in 1930–3 fled in many directions, including east to China's Xinjiang region. Nobody is sure about the numbers, for many died en route, but one reliable source estimates 200,000 (Ohayon, 2006; Polian, 2006; Cameron, 2018). Despite the beefing up of the border patrol along the western frontier, crossings occurred there as well. Karelian peasants fleeing collectivization and Finns who had originally "hopped" the border to cross *into* the Soviet Union but had changed their minds braved thickly forested, swampy, and lake-strewn terrain to make it to the other side. Among Finnish North Americans who retained their original passports, an estimated 1,300 to 1,500 reversed direction between 1931 and 1935. Documented instances of those obtaining assistance from embassies to leave the country later in the 1930s are few and far between (Gelb, 1993: 1098–1101; Saramo, 2022: 124).

Second-wave emigres consisted of Soviet POWs and *Ostarbeiter* (eastern workers conscripted by the Nazis for forced labor) who did not repatriate at the end of the Second World War plus those from countries (re)absorbed within the Soviet Union as the Red Army advanced westward. Most spent time – several years, in many cases – in DP displaced persons camps in Central Europe run by the United Nations Relief and Rehabilitation Administration and its successor organization, the International Relief Organization. Unlike the millions who did repatriate, they resisted Soviet efforts to reclaim them. Fear of reprisal for collaborating with the enemy undoubtedly played a large role in their calculations (Polian, 2002). Their anti-Soviet outlook and indisputable whiteness enhanced their cases for refugee status and their welcome in the West.

The displaced persons camps also contained survivors of the Holocaust, who included Soviet Jews. Although a party of 1,200 Soviet Jews figured among those arriving in the new state of Israel in 1948, Jewish emigration from the USSR remained small throughout the 1950s and 1960s. The Six-Day War in 1967 did encourage interest in making *Aliyah*. So did the Soviet practice of imposing quotas on the admission of Jews to educational institutions and to certain professions as well as an upsurge of popular anti-Semitism, both of which could be connected with Israel's victory. Official Israeli data indicate an upswing in Soviet Jews arriving in the early 1970s, and, by the end of the decade, they numbered 150,000 (Total Immigration to Israel from the Former Soviet Union, 1948–Present). At the same time, and especially after 1974, Soviet Jewish emigration to the United States increased. In fact, by the late 1970s, roughly twice as many Soviet Jews were going to the United States as to Israel (Tolts, 2019, unpublished). Would-be emigrants, however, faced numerous obstacles in obtaining exit visas. So frequently were applications unsuccessful that an entire cohort of applicants received the popular designation of "refuseniks" (*otkazniki*). Exit visas also came at a steep price, thanks to the imposition of exit and "diploma" taxes designed to prevent a "brain drain."

Substantial numbers of other Soviet national minorities took advantage of similar policies based on descent (*jus sanguinis*), previous residency, and linguistic or cultural familiarity. Between 1950 and 1987, the Federal Republic of Germany absorbed 1.4 million Aussiedler – people of German descent from Eastern Europe and the Soviet Union. Most left Poland and Romania, but some 110,000 emigrated from the USSR (Spevack, 1995: 73). From where in the USSR? According to the 1989 census, almost a million of the Soviet Union's 2.04 million ethnic Germans lived in Kazakhstan, mainly descendants of those banished to special settlements at the beginning of the Great Patriotic War. Germans in the RSFSR numbered 842,000 with concentrations in the Altai and Omsk regions of Siberia. Restrictions on where Germans could live and what they could do, which persisted until the early 1970s, help explain considerably higher levels of rural residence – 51 percent in Kazakhstan – and lower levels of education than the average in the USSR (Savoskul, 2016).

The Cold War politics of these decades produced another category of emigrants, namely defectors whose daring escapes from behind the Iron Curtain became grist for the mills of Western propagandists. From ballet dancers Nureyev and Baryshnikov to Stalin's daughter who walked into the US embassy in New Delhi in 1967, to conductor Kiril Kondrashin, and several ice-skating stars, prominent Soviet citizens leveraged their fame by making the "leap to freedom." But less-famous defectors (or would-be defectors) outnumbered them, fleeing Communist oppression by ship across the Black Sea or commandeering one in the South China Sea, exiting through a consular window in New York or otherwise escaping while abroad, and hijacking airplanes. In historian Erik Scott's analysis, they not only created Cold War confrontations but also helped to clarify contrasting international migration regimes. Terms such as "international waters" and "air piracy" took on new dimensions thanks to these Cold War defectors (Scott, 2023).

In the late 1980s, as Mikhail Gorbachev's reforms disrupted the Soviet planned economy without providing any stabilizing mechanisms, life became more precarious, producing a fourth wave of emigration that continued beyond the end of the Soviet Union. The volume of departures ballooned. Jewish emigration to Israel during the years 1990 and 1991 totaled 333,000, an all-time high. It thereafter averaged slightly more than 60,000 per annum for the remainder of the millennium. Ukraine led all former Soviet republics as the country from which Jews left, followed by the Russian Federation. Large numbers of

Bukharan Jews, the ethnoreligious designation referring to Jews from Central Asia, also emigrated in these years, choosing Israel as their prime destination. Between 1989 and 2001, 114,700 made their way to that country. During the same period, Germany overtook the United States as former Soviet Jews' second-most favored destination. The United States absorbed more than 250,000 between 1989 and 1997, but numbers dwindled thereafter (Tolts, 2019: 2, 4).

As in the case of Jews, large numbers of Soviet Germans reacted to the collapse of the economy and then the USSR itself by responding positively to the open invitation from their "home" country. Acting on the principle of *deutsches Volkstum* (German belonging), more than 2 million Germans from the former Soviet Union became German citizens in the fifteen years from 1989 to 2004, with the greatest concentration in the mid-1990s. As many described in post hoc interviews, they left "as entire family clans," settling in clusters (Spevack, 1995: 72, 80, 82, 85; Savoskul, 2016). From the mid-1990s, the volume of German emigrants declined, not due to an improvement in their situation, but rather because of a tightening of cultural and linguistic requirements for entry into Germany (Polian, 2006).

The recent history of Soviet Greeks (Russopontians) combines elements of what happened to the nationalities deported during the 1940s and Soviet Jews and Germans. Removed from Crimea in 1944 and the Caucasus in 1949, many of the several hundred thousand Soviet Greeks indigenous to those areas returned to their former homes in the post-Stalin decades. The political and economic instability occasioned by the implosion of the Soviet Union and active intervention by the Greek government to rescue some 15,000 Greeks from civil strife and economic hardship in Georgia's northwestern province of Abkhazia paved the way for the "repatriation" to Greece of more than 150,000 by the end of the millennium (Diamanti-Karanou, 2003). Settling in eastern Macedonia and Thrace, they inevitably became subjects of jokes and stereotypes mostly based on their dialects.

Finally, Finnish president Mauno Koivisto committed his country in 1990 to offering immigrant status to Ingrian Finns in the spirit of righting an historic wrong, namely the return of 55,000 Ingrians to Soviet jurisdiction in 1944 (Prindiville, 2015: 132–9). Among the estimated 30,000 who seized this opportunity was Sakhalin-born Irina Lukka. While studying Japanese at Leningrad University in the late 1970s, Irina met "a boy" from Estonia whose ethnic origins were Ingrian Finnish. They married and moved to Estonia's famous university town of Tartu in 1980. Eleven years later, as the curtain came down on the Soviet Union, they relocated to Helsinki, where Irina became the director of the Slavonic Division of Finland's National Library (Lukka, interview with author, July 14–15, 2010).

Some streams of migration had their own impetus and trajectories in the years of the fourth wave. We are thinking in particular of human trafficking, one of the most dispiriting consequences of economic distress, familial crisis, and the collapse of the social safety net that accompanied the end of the Soviet Union. The term "human trafficking" has broad applicability. For our purposes, forced labor, debt bondage, and sex trafficking are the most relevant. While most people celebrated the end of Soviet-era restrictions, their disappearance and the insufficiency of law enforcement created ideal conditions for human trafficking of all kinds. When it comes to sex trafficking, a Russian journalist reported in 2006 the "mindboggling figure" of 60,000 women trapped in the trade each year, 90 percent of whom were under twenty-five years old. Reminiscent of the moral panic about the White Slave Trade at the turn of the twentieth century, the entry of so many "Natashas" into a market for sex that previously engaged mainly Asian and African women heightened concern among global organizations. Trafficking thrived especially where prostitution was legal (e.g., the Netherlands and Germany) and Slavic women were considered most desirable (Danilkin, 2006).

Promised glamorous and well-paying jobs, Russian women also traveled to neighboring Turkey, Eastern Europe, Italy, France, Britain, and North America. From the Russian Far East, women were trafficked to China, Japan, and Thailand. Armenian and Azerbaijani women took routes to Saudi Arabia, the United Arab Emirates, Turkey, and Israel. In addition, internal trafficking within post-Soviet space took Ukrainians and Central Asians to Moscow and Petersburg, whence some were sold again. Inevitably, public attention focused on the most wrenching tales of victimization (Buckley, 2009: 121). The 2002 Swedish film *Lilya 4-Ever*, for example, was based on the story of a Lithuanian girl whose mother had decamped to the United States, leaving her vulnerable to a trafficker who lured her to Sweden. There, she committed suicide (Moodysson, 2002).

Of course, not all women who left the former USSR were ensnared by traffickers. The severe economic crisis, however, pushed many into the well-documented rising tide of women among international migrants, some of whom took up sex work (Kofman et al., 2000). The Kazakh woman interviewed by Gülçür and Ilkkaracan offers insight into the choices at hand: as a graduate with a degree in economics, Vera was unable to find work. At age thirty-one, dependent on her parents, she chose to head for Istanbul, a destination popular for low transportation costs, a sizeable migrant community, and a lack of visa requirements. Work in a carpet shop rendered little pay, so when a woman friend suggested prostitution would be much more remunerative, Vera turned to sex work and saved enough to buy a house in Kazakhstan. Still unable to find work at home, she returned to Istanbul (Gülçür and Ilkkaracan, 2002: 415). While many male emigrants took on unskilled labor jobs in construction and the like, other women sought employment in the long-standing migrant specialty of care work. Employment as a nanny, a caregiver, or a domestic servant reduced or eliminated the cost of room and board and offered protection from forces outside the employer's household. Unfortunately, many incidents attest to a nearly total absence of protection from abuse within the household.

Turkey crops up with remarkable frequency as the destination of women from Central Asia and elsewhere from the former Soviet Union. One source claims that roughly twice as many women as men from Uzbekistan migrated there between 2011 and 2019, but the ratio and total numbers are even greater in the case of Georgians (Nurdinova, forthcoming). Uzbeks, Tajiks, Kyrgyz, and Turkmens share with Turks a Muslim culture as well as linguistic proximity, but Georgians have the advantage of a shared border and, thanks to agreements concluded between respective governments in 2006, 2011, and 2015, travel across it does not require a passport and is inexpensive. Most Georgian women interviewed in Ankara for a recent study, arrived by bus and got jobs in domestic service through friends, relatives, or employment agencies. Thanks to live-in conditions, they earn enough to support their families whom they are able to visit frequently (Kocaoglu-Dündar, 2021).

A case can be made – and we have made it elsewhere – for considering soldiers and other military personnel as "militarized migrant communities" when they are mobilized to cross international borders and occupy territory (Siegelbaum and Moch, 2014: 187–8). Thus, Russia's "little green men" crossing into Crimea and Donbas in February–March 2014 to assist in the detachment of those territories from Ukraine could be said to have participated in a form of migration. Regardless of how we conceive of such actions, they usually – as demonstrated by the Wehrmacht crossing into Soviet territory in 1941, or, to cite a more recent example, Russian forces deployed against the Chechen *independistas* during the 1990s – precipitate the displacement of civilians from contested areas, which is more conventionally understood as the migration of refugees.

How many? In November 2014, the *New York Times* reported that "though exact estimates vary . . . roughly 1.5 million people" had left rebel-held territory in eastern Ukraine out of a prewar population of 4.5 million. The question of where they went – how many the Russian Federation absorbed and how many were "internally displaced persons" (IDPs) within Ukraine – became part of the war itself, each side exaggerating the numbers for its own purposes. The Russian delegate to the United Nations High Commissioner for Refugees (UNHCR) claimed already in August 2014 that 730,000 had fled the Donbas for his country, a figure that rose to 810,000 a month later. For his part, Ukrainian observer Klymenko reported to the same body in October 2016 that 1.7 million residents of Crimea and the Donbas, including 170,000 children, had registered as IDPs. He thanked the European Union for its material assistance, but claimed more was necessary (Kramer, 2014, A4; United Nations General Assembly, 2016, 4–5).

This standoff continued for eight years – eight years of dislocations, internal and otherwise, but in either case making for more diasporas – until February 24, 2022. "Not since World War II" is a phrase much repeated since the Russian invasion of Ukraine. The comparison is cold comfort for Ukrainians experiencing conditions not unlike what their parents, grandparents, and great-grandparents went through in 1941–5. And the numbers game continues. In June 2022, the UNHCR heard one delegate after another condemn Russia for its unprovoked invasion of Ukraine that caused, according to the Australian delegate, "over a third" of the population to be displaced and "over 6.3 million" to leave the country. Each tried to outdo the other in demonstrating their country's commitment to accommodate refugees – frontline Moldavia had "received half a million refugees ... of whom 76,000 were opting to remain ... with local families"; Austria "had enabled 400,000 ... to enter the country," of whom 78,000 had decided to stay; Britain had issued 93,000 visas; Portugal was hosting 45,000 Ukrainians, including 13,000 children, and giving "particular attention" to "preventing human trafficking." Turkey, if not frontline then nearby, had welcomed "more than" 202,000, but this was "in addition to the more than four million refugees it was already hosting from various other regions, all of whom received the necessary protections as well as the country's customary hospitality" (United Nations General Assembly, 2022: 2, 5–8, 10).

The UNHCR did not hear from the delegates from Poland or Germany – countries that both would accept more than a million Ukrainian refugees by November 2022. But after everyone else had had their say, "Mr. Atroshenko," the Russian delegate, took the floor to announce that since February 18, "over 2 million people had decided to flee to Russia" because of "the actions of the Kyiv regime, which eight years ago launched an armed internal conflict ... with an influx of Western armaments ... keeping people trapped in populated areas." He assured his listeners that "all entrants into Russia were accorded financial and psychological assistance, medical care ... and schooling for children." For what it is worth, the German database company Statista lists Russia at the top of its table of countries that recorded refugees from Ukraine, with more than 2.8 million, more than Poland and Germany combined (United Nations General Assembly, 2022: 18; Statista Research Department, 2023).

As of this writing, the war in Ukraine casts a pall over the entire world, not only spewing out refugees to all corners of Europe but also raising the specter of a wider, even nuclear war. Let us, therefore, conclude our analysis of the making of diasporas in Soviet and post-Soviet space by citing what we consider a hopeful development. Dateline: "BISHKEK, Kyrgyzstan." There, the *New York Times'* Andrew Higgins reported in October 2022, "rents are sky-rocketing, luxury hotels and grimy hostels do not have beds to spare," and "bands of young migrants, nearly all men, wander aimlessly, dazed at their world turned upside down." Why is this a hopeful sign? We certainly are not oblivious to the wrenching decisions these draft-age men had to make about whether to be "dragooned into fighting in Ukraine" or take up residence in "a country long scorned in Russia as a source of cheap labor and for its backward ways." What gives us hope is that this "vast exodus of Russians" not only to Kyrgyzstan and elsewhere in Central Asia but also to Georgia, Armenia, and Turkey will sap the Russian *silovki* (those from the armed forces, police, security, and intelligence organs) of their thirst for war (Higgins, 2022).

Strictly in terms of migration history, the "chaotic rush for the exit" of what one observer in Moscow estimated as "at least two times bigger" than the number mobilized represents an inversion of the Ukrainian refugee profile – not women, children, and the elderly running away from an invading army, but mostly young men refusing to join it (Kagarlitsky, 2022). Writing history while it is happening is uncomfortable. To whom shall we give the last word? To twenty-five-year-old Dmitri Georgiev from Moscow, now in Georgia, who says, "We joke here that we're creating a 'Little Moscow' and a 'Little Petersburg?'" Or to Aldar, a Buryat accountant who, because the war in Ukraine "doesn't make any sense," fled to neighboring Mongolia even though Buryatia is "where the soul of the Buryat lives"? Or to Vasily Sonkin, thirty-two and also from Moscow who, now residing in Kyrgyzstan, observed that "It is a vaccination against imperialism to come here and be accepted by the Kyrgyz after the way they have been treated in Moscow, never mind other cities" (Higgins, 2022; On Point, 2022; Russian Ethnic Minorities Flee to Mongolia, 2022).

Conclusions

The Soviet Union, a state made up of ethnoterritorial units, contained diasporas in its midst wherever groups of a particular nationality lived outside their homeland. Migrations are what made these national diasporas. Did this matter? The answer partly depends on what propelled people away from their national homelands. For those who sought and attained a better life elsewhere, the improvement may have outweighed the costs of dislocation. For the punished or mistrusted, longing for the relative normality of their original homeland tended to persist. Many coercively relocated national groups eventually did return to their homelands, although three (Crimean Tatars, Volga Germans, and Meskhetian Turks) waited in vain, their homelands permanently obliterated from the map.

Diasporas were internal until they weren't – that is, until the Soviet Union ceased to exist. At that point, fifteen newly independent nation-states – the former Union republics – exercised varying degrees of accommodating national minorities. Economic turbulence, questions of citizenship, civil rights, and language usage provoked anxiety, persuading large numbers of such minorities to "return" to their national homelands. Such crossing of borders, previously pro forma, now meant engaging in international travel, albeit within the CIS, formed in December 1991. The Russian diaspora, the largest within the former Soviet Union, shrank the most, as millions left Kazakhstan, Kyrgyzstan, Ukraine, Moldavia, and the newly independent Baltic states. Other national groups relocated as well, discomforted by changes in legal and social status. They were not necessarily absorbed within their national homelands, but – for a variety of reasons – joined diasporic communities in the Russian Federation, another former Soviet republic, or in the "far abroad."

For those who identified with national homelands outside the former Soviet Union (Germans, Greeks, Jews), emigration held a strong attraction, especially in the years surrounding 1991. Actually, people had been emigrating from – and immigrating to – the Soviet Union since its formation in 1922, and that history too is part of the making and unmaking of diasporas. The October Revolution and the dream of building socialism attracted political sympathizers from near and far. During the 1930s, refugees from fascism arrived, including the Spanish *niños*, and, after the Second World War, Armenian repatriates. As far as ethnic Russians are concerned, rejoining compatriots in the Motherland appealed to those resident in China (especially after 1949), and in post-Soviet times, after the introduction of a program facilitating the move.

Wars hot and cold spurred the first three waves of emigration: the White émigrés of the civil war years; the nonreturning POWs, *Ostarbeiters*, and displaced persons in the aftermath of the Great Patriotic War; and the Cold War's defectors. If the fourth wave of emigration around the time of the Soviet Union's demise was driven largely by economic and social instabilities, then what might be described as a fifth wave definitely was war-related and most clearly illustrates the post-Soviet consequences of diasporas made in the Soviet years.

In the Donbas, where ethnic and linguistic lines between Ukrainian and Russian blurred over several generations, Ukraine's Maidan Revolution generated divisions even within families into pro- and anti-separatist camps. For the next eight years, as Russian and Ukrainian forces faced off against each other, residents hunkered down, emigrated eastward to Russia, or fled westward into the Ukrainian interior. Russia's invasion of Ukraine in 2022 precipitated even larger migration flows into Russia, some of it coerced. At the same time, Ukrainians formed a new diaspora of millions primarily in Eastern and Central Europe. Finally, the Russian army's attempts to draft new soldiers prompted a large exodus of young men, notably to former Soviet republics such as Georgia and Kyrgyzstan.

Not all post-Soviet consequences of Soviet era migrations have been as dolorous. The establishment of national quotas in universities, exchanges of personnel between factories of the same type, the provision of dormitories for urban newcomers, and other Soviet practices facilitated multinational friendships. Encountering each other in Soviet industrial, governmental, and educational institutions, citizens of different ethnic backgrounds, including diasporic national groups, often fell in love and decided to marry. Although such couples sometimes faced resistance from their own families, in the long run, they helped overcome mutual ignorance and erode national prejudices. The Soviet Union was not the only empire containing national diasporas in its midst, although the making of those diasporas often bore the stamp of "Made in the USSR." It is still too soon to tell whether the postimperial consequences will be positive.

References

AFP (2021). Russia Eyes Measures to Tackle Migrant Labor Shortage. *Moscow Times*, February 10. www.themoscowtimes.com/2021/02/10/russia-eyes-measures-to-tackle-migrant-labor-shortage-a72894 (accessed March 7, 2023).

Akimov, Server. (2009). http://iremember.ru/partizani/akimov-server/stranitsa-2.html (accessed September 24, 2022).

Austin, L. (2023). From Internationalism to Displacement: Minoritized Communities in the Formerly Soviet Southern Tier. PhD dissertation, Michigan State University.

Bachmann, B. (1983). *Memories of Kazakhstan: A Report on the Life Experiences of a German Woman in Russia*. Lincoln, NE: American Historical Society of Germans from Russia.

Bekirov, Alim Uspenovich. (2009). http://iremember.ru/zenitchiki/bekirov-alim-useinovich.html (accessed September 24, 2022).

Berdinskikh, V. A. (2005). *Spetsposelentsy: Politicheskaia ssylka narodov Sovetskoi Rossii*. Moscow: Novoe literaturnoe obozrenie.

Bernstein, S. and Cherny, R. W. (2014). Searching for the Soviet Dream: Prosperity and Disillusionment on the Soviet Seattle Agricultural Commune, 1922–1927. *Agricultural History*, 88 (1), 22–44.

Brown, K. (2003). *A Biography of No Place: From Ethnic Borderland to Soviet Heartland*. Cambridge, MA: Harvard University Press.

Brown, K. (2013). *Plutopia: Nuclear Families, Atomic Cities, and the Great Soviet and American Plutonium Disasters*. Oxford: Oxford University Press.

Brubaker, R. (1995). Aftermaths of Empire and the Unmixing of People: Historical and Comparative Perspectives. *Ethnic & Racial Studies*, 18 (2), 189–218.

Buckley, M. (2009). Human Trafficking in the Twenty-First Century: Implications for Russia, Europe, and the World. In L. Racioppi and K. O'Sullivan See, eds., *Gender Politics in Post-Communist Eurasia*. East Lansing: Michigan State University Press, 119–45.

Bugai, N. F. (1995). *L. Beriia – I. Stalinu: "Soglasno Vashemu ukazaniiu . . ."*. Moscow: AIRO-XX.

Bugai, N. F., and Gonov, A. M. (1998). *Kavkaz: Narody v eshelonakh (20–60-e gody)*. Moscow: Insan.

Byl' ukraintsem, stal russkim. Kto byl' Brezhnev po natsional'nosti? https://zen.yandex.ru/media/obistorii/nacionalnosti-5e8dc8c43c7302489cd3effb (accessed September 25, 2022).

Cameron, S. (2018). *The Hungry Steppe: Famine, Violence, and the Making of Soviet Kazakhstan*. Ithaca, NY: Cornell University Press.

Chelokhaeva, Rasmie Zkimovna. (2009). http://iremember.ru/grazhdanskie/che lokhaeva-rasmie-akimovna.html (accessed September 25, 2022).

Chukovskaya, L. (1994). *The Akhmatova Journals*, vol. 1. New York: Farrar, Straus & Giroux.

Daneliya, G. dir. (1977). *Mimino*. Mosfil'm.

Danilkin, A. (2006). Zhenu otdai diade . . . *Trud*. March 21.

Danilov, V. P., Manning, R., and Viola, L. (1999–2006). *Tragediia sovetskoi derevni: Kollektivizatsiia i razkulachivanie: Dokumenty i materialy v 5 tomakh, 1927–1939*, 5 vols. Moscow: ROSSPEN.

Diamanti-Karanou, P. (2003). Migration of Ethnic Greeks from the Former Soviet Union to Greece, 1990–2000: Policy Decisions and Implications. *Southeast European and Black Sea Studies*, 3 (1), 25–45.

Donets, E., and Chudinovskikh, O. (2020). Russian Policy on Assistance to the Resettlement of Compatriots against the Background of International Experience. *Population and Economics*, 4 (3), 1–32.

Duc, D. M., Hieu, N. C., and Hung, T. D. (2022). Cooperation between Vietnam and Russia in the Field of Labor Migration: Directions and New Opportunities. *DEMIS. Demographic Research*, 2 (1), 191–202.

Eaton, N. (2020). Provisional Redemption and the Fate of Kaliningrad's Germans. *Kritika: Explorations in Russian and Eurasian History*, 21 (1), 41–72.

Edgar, A. (2022). *Intermarriage and the Friendship of Peoples: Ethnic Mixing in Soviet Central Asia*. Ithaca, NY: Cornell University Press.

Fierman, W. (1991). Central Asian Youth and Migration. In W. Fierman, ed., *Soviet Central Asia: The Failed Transformation*. Boulder, CO: Westview Press.

Fiore, V. (2017). A Toxic, Closed-Off City on the Edge of the World. *The Atlantic*, November 8. www.theatlantic.com/video/index/545228/my-deadly-beautiful-city-norilsk (accessed September 21, 2022).

Friedgut, T. (1989). *Iuzovka and Revolution: Life and Work in Russia's Donbass, 1869–1924*. Princeton, NJ: Princeton University Press.

Gelb, M. (1993). Karelian Fever: The Finnish Immigrant Community during Stalin's Purges. *Europe-Asia Studies*, 45 (6), 1091–1116.

Gelb, M. (1995). An Early Soviet Ethnic Deportation: The Far Eastern Koreans. *Russian Review*, 54 (3), 389–412.

German, A. A., and Kurochkin, A. N. (1998). *Nemtsy v SSSR v "Trudovoi armii": 1941–1945*. Moscow: Gotika.

Ginsburgs, G. (1989). The Case of Vietnamese Gastarbeiters in the Soviet Union. *Osteuropa-Recht*, H3, 166–87.

Goff, K. (2020). *Nested Nationialisms: Making and Unmaking Nations in the Soviet Caucasus*. Ithaca, NY: Cornell University Press.

Goff, K. (2022). Postwar Rebuilding and Resettlements in the Soviet Union: A Case of Azeri Migration. *Slavic Review*, 81 (1), 97–121.

Goldman, W. (2022). The War Economy: Central Asian Workers and Labor Mobilization. Industrious Nations: Reconsidering Nationality and Economy in the Soviet Union Workshop, Princeton University.

Gosudarstvennyi Arkhiv Rossiiskoi Federatsii (GARF), f. 327, op. 1, d. 2, d. 90; op. 2, d. 441, d. 442.

Gülçür, L., and Ilkkaracan, P. (2002). The "Natasha" Experience: Migrant Sex Workers from the Former Soviet Union and Eastern Europe in Turkey. *Women's Studies International Forum*, 25 (4), 411–21.

Gur'ianov, A. E. (1997). *Repressii protiv poliakov i pol'skikh grazhdan*. Moscow: Zven'ia.

Halavach, D. (2021). Unsettling Borderlands: The Population Exchange and the Polish Minority in Soviet Belarus, 1944–1947. ASEEES Convention.

Hamed-Troyansky, V. (2021). Muslim Return Migration from the Middle East to Russia, 19–21C. University of California–Santa Barbara Global Studies Colloquium Series, unpublished paper.

Higgins, A. (2022). Russians Find Refuge in Country They Scorned. *New York Times*, October 5, A1, 8.

Holley, D. (2005). In Russia's Far East, a Jewish Revival. *Los Angeles Times*, August 7.

Itogi perepisi 2001 goda na Ukraine (2003). *Demoskop Weekly*, no. 113–14, May 19–June 1. www.demoscope.ru/weekly/2003/0113/analit03.php. (accessed May 12, 2022).

Ivakhnyuk, I. (2009). *The Russian Migration Policy and Its Impact on Human Development: The Historical Perspective*. New York: United Nations.

Kaiser, C. P. (2019). What Are they Doing? After All, We're Not Germans. In K. A. Goff and L. H. Siegelbaum, eds., *Empire and Belonging in the Eurasian Borderlands*. Ithaca, NY: Cornell University Press, 80–94.

Kagarlitsky, B. (2022). Russia Is Losing the War. *Democracy Now!* December 8. www.democracynow.org (accessed February 26, 2023).

Keller, B. (1989). Soviet Nationalist Violence Spreads to Uzbek Republic. *New York Times*, June 5, A6.

Kendall, E. (2013). *Balanchine and the Lost Muse: Revolution and the Making of a Choreographer*. Oxford: Oxford University Press.

Khanga, Y. (1992). *Soul to Soul: A Black Russian Jewish Woman's Search for Her Roots*. New York: W. W. Norton.

Kheifets, L. (1955). *Pereseliates' k nam na Sakhalin.* Iuzhno-Sakhalinsk: Pereselencheskii otdel pri Sakhalinskom oblispolkome.

King, C. (2000). *The Moldovans: Romania, Russia, and the Politics of Culture.* Stanford, CA: Hoover Institution Press.

Kirss, T. and Hinrikus, R. eds. (2009). *Estonian Life Stories.* Budapest: Central European University Press.

Kocaoglu-Dündar, B. (2021). Georgian Immigrant Women in Turkey: Ankara Case. *Antropoloji* 42: 19–26. https://doi.org/10.33613/antropolojidergisi .1001365 (accessed November 6, 2022).

Kofman, E., Phizacklea, A., Raghuram, P., and Sales, R. (2000). *Gender and International Migration in Europe.* London: Routledge.

Kokaisl, P. (2018). Koreans in Central Asia: A Different Korean Nation. *Asian Ethnicity,* 19 (2), 1–25.

Kolotnecha, O. (2007). Osobaia fermerskaia zona. https://expert.ru/northwest/ 2007/37/derevnya_lesnaya (accessed September 25, 2020).

Kommunisticheskaia partiia Sovetskogo Soiuza (1983–90). *KPSS v rezoliutsiiakh i resheniiakh s"ezdov, konferentsii i plenumov TsK.* 9th ed. Moscow: Izd-vo polit. Litry, 12: 405.

Konov, V. (1974). Prodolzhenie sleduet... *Sel'skaia molodezh,* 4, 12–18.

Korobkov, A. (2008). Post-Soviet Migration: New Trends at the Beginning of the Twenty-First Century. In C. J. Buckley, B. A. Ruble, and E. Trouth Hofmann, eds., *Migration, Homeland, and Belonging in Eurasia.* Baltimore, MD: Johns Hopkins University Press, 69–79.

Kotkin, S. (1993). Peopling Magnitostroi: The Politics of Demography. In W. Rosenberg and L. H. Siegelbaum, eds., *Social Dimensions of Soviet Industrialization.* Bloomington: Indiana University Press, 63–104.

Kramer, A. (2014). Nowhere to Run in Eastern Ukraine. *New York Times,* November 14, A4.

Lahusen, T. (1997). *How Life Writes the Book: Real Socialism and Socialist Realism in Stalin's Russia.* Ithaca, NY: Cornell University Press.

Lam, K. (2010). Forging a Socialist Homeland from Multiple Worlds: North American Finns in Soviet Karelia 1921–1938. *Revista Română pentru Studii Baltice și Nordice,* 2 (2), 203–24.

Laycock, J. (2009). The Repatriation of Armenians to Soviet Armenia, 1945–49. In P. Gatrell and N. Baron, eds., *Warlands: Population Resettlement and State Reconstruction in the Soviet-East European Borderlands, 1945–50.* Houndmills: Palgrave Macmillan, 140–61.

Lehmann, M. (2012). A Different Kind of Brothers: Exclusion and Partial Integration after Repatriation to a Soviet "Homeland." *Ab Imperio,* (3), 171–211.

Lieven, A. (1999). *Chechnya: Tombstone of Russian Power*. New Haven, CT: Yale University Press.

Lively, P. (1987). *Moon Tiger*. New York: Grove Press.

Lukacs (2013). *Stanford Encyclopedia of Philosophy*. https://plato.stanford.edu/entries/lukacs (accessed October 20, 2022).

Meskhetian Turks. *Wikipedia*. https://en.wikipedia.org/wiki/Meskhetian_Turks (accessed September 21, 2022).

Makarov, A. (1974). Vysota. *Sel'skaia molodezh*, 3, 22–5.

Makarov, V. G., and Khristoforov, V. S. (2003). Passazhiry "Filosofskogo parokhoda" (sud'by intelligentsii, represirovannoi letom-oseniu 1922 g.). *Voprosy filosofii*, (7), 113–37.

Manchester, L. (2007). Repatriation to a Totalitarian Homeland: The Ambiguous Alterity of Russian Repatriates from China to the USSR. *Diaspora: A Journal of Transnational Studies*, 16 (3), 353–88.

Manley, R. (2009). *To the Tashkent Station: Evacuation and Survival in the Soviet Union at War*. Ithaca, NY: Cornell University Press.

Mantsetov, N. V. (1964). Sblizhenie natsii i vozniknovenie internatsional'noi obshchnosti narodov v SSSR. *Voprosy istorii*, (5), 38–53.

Martin, T. (2001). *Affirmative Action Empire: Nations and Nationalism in the Soviet Union, 1923–1939*. Ithaca, NY: Cornell University Press.

Maslov, V., Baranova, E., and Lopatin, M. (2022). "Nam udalos' perevezti mebel' i dazhe korovu, ovets i koz": Lichnoe imushchestvo sel'skikh pereselentsev, priekhavshikh v Kaliningradskuiu oblast' v 1946 godu. *Zhurnal frontirnykh issledovanii*, 3: 34–62.

Matley, I. (1979). The Dispersal of the Ingrian Finns. *Slavic Review*, 38 (1), 1–16.

Moodysson, L. dir. (2002). *Lilya 4-ever*. Sonet Film.

Morray, J. P. (1983). *Project Kuzbas: American Workers in Siberia, 1921–1926*. New York: International.

Natsional'nost' – noril'chane. (2020). www.ttelegraf.ru/projects/tsifryi-i-fak tyi/nacionalnost-norilchane (accessed September 21, 2022).

Nornickel. (2022). www.nornickel.com (accessed September 5, 2022).

Nurdinova, S. (forthcoming). Uzbek migrants in Turkey: Gender, Satisfaction in Turkey, and Return Intentions. *REGION: Regional Studies of Russia, Eastern Europe, and Central Asia*.

Ohayon, I. (2006). *La sédentarisation des Kazakhs dans l'URSS de Staline: Collectivisation et changement social (1928–1945)*. Paris: Maisonneuve et Larose Institut français d'etudes sr l'Asie Centrale.

On Point (2022). National Public Radio. October 25.

Pallot, J., and Piacentini, L. (2012). *Gender, Geography, and Punishment: The Experience of Women in Central Russia*. Oxford: Oxford University Press.

Paxton, R. (2007). Arctic Mosque Stays Open but Muslim Numbers Shrink. Reuters, April 15. www.reuters.com/article/us-muslims-russia-arctic-idUSL107249362007041 (accessed September 5, 2022).

Pereltsvaig, A. (2014). Birobidzhan: Frustrated Dreams of a Jewish Homeland. *Languages of the World.* www.languagesoftheworld.info (accessed October 11, 2022).

Pereseliates' v zapadnyi Kazakhstan (1960). Ural'sk.

Pervaia vseobshchaia perepis' naseleniia Rossiiskoi imperii. (1905). *Demoskop Weekly*, no. 987–8. www.demoscope.ru/weekly/ssp/rus_lan_97.php (accessed November 1, 2022).

Peyrouse, S. (2007). Nationhood and the Minority Question in Central Asia: The Russians in Kazakhstan. *Europe-Asia Studies*, 59 (3), 481–501.

Pobol', N. I., and Polian, P. M. (2005). *Stalinskie deportatsii, 1928–1953 gg.* Moscow: Materik.

Pohl, M. (2007). The "Plant of One Hundred Languages": Ethnic Relations and Soviet Identity in the Virgin Lands. In N. B. Breyfogle, A. Schrader, and W. Sunderland, eds., *Peopling the Russian Periphery: Borderland Colonization in Eurasian History.* London: Routledge, 238–61.

Polian, P. M. (2002). *Zhertvy dvukh diktatur: zhizn', trud, unizhenie i smert' sovetskikh voennoplennykh i ostarbeiterov na chuzhbine i na rodine.* Moscow: ROSSPEN.

Polian, P. M. (2004). *Against Their Will: The History and Geography of Forced Migrations in the USSR.* Budapest: Central European University Press.

Polian, P. (2006). Emigratsiia: kto i kogda v XX veke pokidal Rossiiu. *Demoskop Weekly*, no. 251–2, June 19–August 20. www.demoscope.ru /weekly/2006/0251/analit01.php (accessed October 27, 2022).

Prindiville, N. (2015). The Return of the Ingrian Finns: Ethnicity, Identity and Reforms in Finland's Return Immigration Policy 1990–2010. PhD dissertation, School of Slavonic and East European Studies, University College London.

Qualls, K. (2020), *Stalin's Niños: Educating Spanish Civil War Refugee Children in the Soviet Union, 1937–1951.* Toronto: University of Toronto Press.

Radnitz, S. (2006) Weighing the Political and Economic Motivations for Migration in Post-Soviet Space: The Case of Uzbekistan. *Europe-Asia Studies*, 58 (5), 653–77.

Reeves, M. (2007). Travels in the Margins of the State: Everyday Geography in the Ferghana Valley Borderlands. In J. Sahadeo and R. Zanca, eds., *Everyday Life in Central Asia Past and Present.* Bloomington: Indiana University Press, 281–300.

Rittersporn, G. T. (forthcoming). Lost and Found Revolutions: Between Emancipatory Dreams and Mass Terror in the Soviet Union. In J. A. Getty and L. H. Siegelbaum, eds., *Reflections on Stalinism*. Ithaca, NY: Northern Illinois University Press.

Roman, M. (2002). Making Caucasians Black: Moscow since the Fall of Communism and the Racialization of Non-Russians. *Journal of Communist Studies and Transition Politics*, 18 (2), 1–27.

Russia Hit by Fall in Migrant Workers from Central Asia (2021). *Financial Times*, May 8. www.ft.com/content//c7c17f5e-e7b2-45bb-97d7-d5b456fb2bec (accessed March 5, 2023).

Russian Ethnic Minorities Flee to Mongolia. *Deutsche Welle*, November 22. www.dw.com/en/russian-minorities-flee-to-mongolia-to-avoid-draft/video-63851042 (accessed February 23, 2023).

Sahadeo, J. (2019). *Voices from the Soviet Edge: Southern Migrants in Leningrad and Moscow*. Ithaca, NY: Cornell University Press.

Saramo, S. (2022). *Building That Bright Future: Soviet Karelia in the Life Writing of Finnish North Ameicans*. Toronto: University of Toronto Press.

Savoskul, M. (2016). Vyezd nemtsev iz SSSR i stran SNG i Baltii. *Demoskop Weekly*, no. 681–2, April 4–17. www.demoscope.ru/weekly/2016/0681/tema02.php (accessed October 24, 2020).

Sawyer, B. (2013). American "Know-How" on the Soviet Frontier: Soviet Institutions and American Immigration to the Soviet Union in the Era of the New Economic Policy. PhD dissertation, Michigan State University.

Schlögel, K. (2023). *The Soviet Century: Archeology of a Lost World*. Princeton, NJ: Princeton University Press.

Scott, E. R. (2016). *Familiar Strangers: The Georgian Diaspora and the Evolution of the Soviet Empire*. Oxford: Oxford University Press.

Scott, E. R. (2023). World without Exit: Soviet Cold War Defectors and the Borders of Globalization. Oxford: Oxford University Press.

Scott, J. (1942 [1989]). *Behind the Urals: An American Worker in Russia's City of Steel*. Bloomington: Indiana University Press.

Shulman, E. (2008). *Stalinism on the Frontier of Empire: Women and State Formation in the Soviet Far East*. Cambridge: Cambridge University Press.

Siegelbaum, L. H. (1988). *Stakhanovism and the Politics of Productivity in the USSR, 1935–1941*. Cambridge: Cambridge University Press.

Siegelbaum, L. H. (2008). *Cars for Comrades: The Life of the Soviet Automobile*. Ithaca, NY: Cornell University Press.

Siegelbaum, L. H. (2016). People on the Move during the "Era of Stagnation": The Rural Exodus in the RSFSR during the 1960s–1980s. In D. Fainburg and

A. Kalinovsky, eds., *Reconsidering Stagnation in the Brezhnev Era*. Lanham, MD: Lexington Books, 43–58.

Siegelbaum, L. H. (2017). The "Flood" of 1945: Regimes and Repertoires of Migration in the Soviet Union at War's End. *Social History*, 42 (1), 52–72.

Siegelbaum, L. H. (2019). *Stuck on Communism: Memoir of a Russian Historian*. Ithaca, NY: Northern Illinois University Press.

Siegelbaum, L. H., and Moch, L. P. (2014). *Broad Is My Native Land: Repertoires and Regimes of Migration in Russia's Twentieth Century*. Ithaca, NY: Cornell University Press.

Siegelbaum, L. H., and Moch, L. P. (2016). Transnationalism in One Country? Seeing and Not Seeing Transborder Migration within the Soviet Union. *Slavic Review*, 75 (4), 970–96.

Siegelbaum, L. H., and Walkowitz, D. J. (1995). *Workers of the Donbass Speak: Survival and Identity in the New Ukraine, 1989–1992*, Albany: State University of New York Press.

Snyder, T. (2003). *The Reconstruction of Nations: Poland, Ukraine, Lithuania, Belarus, 1569–1999*. New Haven, CT: Yale University Press.

Spevack, E. (1995). Ethnic Germans from the East: "Aussiedler" in Germany, 1970–1994. *German Politics & Society*, 13 (4), 71–91.

Stadnik, K. (2009). Ukrainian-Polish Population Transfers, 1944–46: Moving in Opposite Directions. In P. Gatrell and N. Baron, eds., *Warlands: Population Resettlement and State Reconstruction in the Soviet-East European Borderlands, 1945–50* Houndmills: Palgrave-Macmillan, 165–87.

Stalino. https://don.fandom.com/ru/wiki/%D0%A1%D1%82%D0%B0%D0% BB%D0%B8%D0%BD%D0%BE# (accessed September 21, 2022).

Stankova, M. (2010). *Georgi Dimitrov: A Life*. London: Tauris.

Statista Research Department. (2023). Estimated Number of Refugees from Ukraine Recorded in Europe and Asia since February 2022 as of May 9, 2023, by Selected Country. www.statista.com/statistics/1312584/ukrainian-refugees-by-country (accessed May 22, 2023).

Stepakov, V. N., and Balashov, E. A. (2001). *V 'novykh raionakh:' Iz istorii osvoeniia karel'skogo peresheika, 1940–1941, 1944–1950 gg*. St. Petersburg: Nordmedizdat.

Suny, R. G. (1993). *The Revenge of the Past: Nationalism, Revolution, and the Collapse of the Soviet Union*. Stanford, CA: Stanford University Press, 1993.

Suny, R. G., and Martin, T. eds. (2001). *A State of Nations: Empire and Nation-Making in the Age of Lenin and Stalin*. Oxford: Oxford University Press.

Susokolov, A. A. (1987). *Mezhnatsional'nye braki v SSSR*. Moscow: Mysl'.

Taubman, W. (2003). *Khrushchev: The Man and His Era*. New York: W. W. Norton.

Time (1934). Austria: Stalin, Schutzbund & Orphans, August 20. https://content .time.com/time/subscriber/article/0,33009,747706,00.html (accessed October 13, 2022).

Tolts, M. (2019). A Half Century of Jewish Emigration from the Former Soviet Union: Demographic Aspects, Project for Russian and Eurasian Jewry, Davis Center for Russian and Eurasian Studies, Harvard University, November.

Total Immigration to Israel from the Former Soviet Union, 1948–Present. Jewish Virtual Library. www.jewishvirtuallibrary.org/total-immigration-to-israel-from-former-soviet-union (accessed March 7, 2023).

United Nations General Assembly (2016). Executive Committee of Programme ... of the High Commissioner for Refugees, 67th session (Geneva), October 5. www.unhcr.org/en-us/excom/excomrep/5906e1d47/ summary-record-of-the-697th-meeting.html (accessed November 7, 2022).

United Nations General Assembly (2022). Executive Committee of Programme ... of the High Commissioner for Refugees, 84th meeting (Geneva), June 28. www.unhcr.org/62bc19e04 (accessed November 7, 2022).

United States Holocaust Memorial Museum (USHMM) (1990) RG-31.053, Memoirs of Abram Tseitlin.

Viola, L. (2001). The Other Archipelago. *Slavic Review*, 60 (4), 730–55.

Vsesoiuznaia perepis' naseleniia 1959 goda: Natsional'nyi sostav naseleniia po respublikam SSSR. *Demoskop Weekly*. www.demoscope.ru (accessed October 6, 2022).

Vsesoiuznaia perepis' naseleniia 1970 goda: Natsional'nyi sostav naseleniia po respublikam SSSR. *Demoskop Weekly*. www.demoscope.ru (accessed October 6, 2022).

Vsesoiuznaia perepis' naseleniia 1989 goda: Natsional'nyi sostav naseleniia po respublikam SSSR. *Demoskop Weekly*. www.demoscope.ru (accessed October 6, 2022).

Williams, C. (2015). Latvia with a Large Minority. *Los Angeles Times*, May 2. www.latimes.com/world/europe/la-fg-latvia-russia-next-20150502-story .html (accessed September 23, 2022).

Woodard, L. (2020). "Yeast for the Russian Land": Envisioning the Return of Primorskii Krai's Old Believers. *REGION: Regional Studies of Russia, Eastern Europe, and Central Asia*, 9 (2), 81–99.

World's Worst Polluted Places: The Top Ten of the Dirty Thirty. A Project of the Blacksmith's Institute (2007). www.worstpolluted.org/reports/file/2007% 20Report%20updated%202009.pdf (accessed September 25, 2022).

Ylikangas, M. (2011). The Sower Commune: An American Finnish Agricultural Utopia in the Soviet Russia. *Journal of Finnish Studies*, 15 (1), 52–85.

Young, Glennys (2014). To Russia with "Spain": Spanish Exiles in the USSR and the Longue Durée of Soviet History. *Kritika: Explorations in Russian and Eurasian History*, 15 (2), 395–419.

Zemskov, V. N. (2003). *Spetsposelentsy v SSSR, 1930–1960*. Moscow: Nauka.

Zevelev, I. (2001). *Russia and Its New Diasporas*. Washington, DC: United States Institute of Peace.

Cambridge Elements ☰

Soviet and Post-Soviet History

Mark Edele

University of Melbourne

Mark Edele teaches Soviet history at the University of Melbourne, where he is Hansen Professor in History and Deputy Dean in the Faculty of Arts. His most recent books are *Stalinism at War* (2021) and *Russia's War Against Ukraine* (2023). He is one of the convenors of the Research Initiative on Post-Soviet Space (RIPSS) at the University of Melbourne.

Rebecca Friedman

Florida International University

Rebecca Friedman is Founding Director of the Wolfsonian Public Humanities Lab and Professor of History at Florida International University in Miami. Her recent book, Modernity, Domesticity and Temporality: Time at Home, supported by the National Endowment for the Humanities, explores modern time and home in twentieth century Russia (2020). She is one of the editors for the Bloomsbury Academic series A Cultural History of Time.

About the Series

Elements in Soviet and Post-Soviet History pluralise the history of the former Soviet space. Contributions decolonise Soviet history and provincialise the former metropole: Russia. In doing so, the series provides an up-to-date history of the present of the region formerly known as the Soviet Union.

Cambridge Elements $^{\equiv}$

Soviet and Post-Soviet History

Elements in the Series

Making National Diasporas: Soviet-Era Migrations and Post-Soviet Consequences
Lewis H. Siegelbaum and Leslie Page Moch

A full series listing is available at: www.cambridge.org/ESPH